Matthew M. Vriends, PhD

Pigeons

Everything About Purchase, Care,
Management, Diet, Diseases, and
Behavior of Pigeons

With a Special Chapter: Understanding Pigeons

With Color Photographs by Well-Known Photographers and
Drawings by Michele Earle-Bridges

New York • London • Toronto • Sydney

Cover photographs
Front: Kings
Inside front cover: Ice pigeon

Inside back cover: Capuchine
Back: above left: Danish tumbler
above right: Double-crested priest
below left: English modena
below right: Hungarian

Photograph credits:
D. Duus: pages 9, 27, 28, 45, 46, 63, back cover; D. J. Hammer: pages 10 top; 64; Steve Holden: front cover; inside back cover; R. Lauwers: inside front cover; M. Ridder: page 10 bottom.

Matthew M. Vriends, the author of this book, is a Dutch-born biologist/ornithologist who holds a number of advanced degrees, including a PhD in zoology. Dr. Vriends has written over eighty books in three languages on birds and other small animals. He has traveled extensively in North and South America, the United States, Africa, Australia, and Europe to observe and study birds and mammals in their natural environment and is widely regarded as an expert in tropical ornithology and aviculture. Dr. Vriends is the author or advisory editor of many of Barron's pet books. He and his family live near Cincinnati, Ohio.

All inquiries should be addressed to:
Barron's Educational Series, Inc.
250 Wireless Boulevard
Hauppauge, NY 11788

International Standard Book No. 0-8120-4044-9

Library of Congress Catalog Card No. 88-22272

Library of Congress Cataloging-in-Publication Data

Vriends, Matthew M., 1937–
    Pigeons: a complete pet owner's manual.

    Includes index.
    1. Pigeons.   I. Title.
SF465.V75   1988   636.5'96   88-22272
ISBN 0-8120-4044-9

PRINTED IN THE UNITED STATES OF AMERICA

901   9770   98765432

A Note of Warning:
The subject of this book is how to take care of various fancy pigeons in captivity. In dealing with these birds, always remember that newly purchased birds — even when they appear perfectly healthy — may well be carriers of salmonellae (see page 51). This is why it is highly advisable to have sample droppings analyzed and to observe strict hygienic rules. Other infectious diseases that can endanger humans, such as ornithosis (see page 50), are common in various pigeons. If you see a doctor because you or a member of your household has symptoms of a cold or of the flu, mention that you keep pigeons. No one who is allergic to feathers or feather dust should keep birds. If you have any doubts, consult your physician before you buy a bird.

Contents

Preface

The earliest mention of pigeon keeping dates from the 4th Egyptian dynasty (about 2600 BC); a "menu" carved in stone describes the Pharaohs' method of cooking pigeons!

Pigeons or doves are mentioned repeatedly in the Bible. The dove that was sent out by Noah to see if the floods were receding, and that returned with an olive twig in its beak, is said by some to have been a tame variety. Though it is not possible to say when humans first started to keep and breed pigeons, we know that the Romans were already experienced breeders, who kept, among others, highfliers and tumblers.

At present, we have over 200 breeds of domesticated pigeons and as many as 1,250 varieties. It is, of course, not possible to describe every breed and variety, but a good cross section will be covered. All the breeds and varieties over about 50 centuries have arisen through generations of selective breeding, from a single species of wild pigeon: the rock dove (*Columba livia*).

I do not pretend to have covered every intricate facet of the hobby, but I have endeavored to give a good general introduction for the prospective pigeon hobbyist as well as one who already keeps pigeons and requires further relevant information. There is ample guidance on suitable housing, on feeding and digestion, as well as a chapter "Understanding Your Pigeon." The selection of breeding pairs, which is very important for the prospective breeder, has also been adequately covered, so that the reader will be able to make an informed choice of breed or variety. Should this book stimulate further investigation of this fascinating hobby, with the help of pigeon organizations and other reading on the subject, it will have served its purpose.

I would like to thank my colleague and friend, Mr. John Coborn, for the work he took from my hands in helping to produce this book. My dear friend, Dr. Alice DeGroot, MS, DVM, of Sandia Park, New Mexico, unselfishly shared experiences and information and took time from her busy schedule to review the manuscript. My wife, Mrs. Lucia Vriends-Parent, also deserves my heartfelt thanks for her continuing positive assistance.

I am, of course, always ready to receive constructive criticisms or recommendations regarding this book.

Loveland, Ohio   Matthew M. Vriends
Fall, 1988

Soyons fidèles à nos faiblesses.
For Larry and Shirley Mohrfield
and Kathy King

Domesticated Pigeons

It is not known where birds were first kept in captivity, but it must have been long before humans expressed themselves in wall paintings or in writing. There is evidence in the cultural history of both the old and the new worlds that birds were kept by many different peoples. Paintings and hieroglyphics left behind by the ancient Egyptians contain many references to pigeons, parrots, ducks, and ibises, as well as other birds used for hunting.

In the Near East, the pigeon seems to have established itself as a common garden or park bird in ancient times. Today the total number of pigeons cannot even be estimated. The pigeon has been used for various purposes for thousands of years: messenger services, food, and decoration. Pigeon racing has become a worldwide sport.

The Pigeon Fancy

The Greek philosopher Aristotle (384–322 BC) wrote the first report about "pigeon sport," and in Athens at that time, pigeons were already used as messengers. The fact that pigeons, like many bird species, instinctively return to their place of birth, or where they feel at home, was exploited by the ancient Orientals. The people of Baghdad, for example, had the first messenger service to the Syrians and the Persians. In 1150, the Sultan of Baghdad introduced a pigeon postal service that functioned until about 1258, when Baghdad fell to the Mongols. In the 16th century, Prince William of Orange of the Netherlands used pigeons during the 80-year war to carry messages to beleaguered towns such as Leyden and Haarlem. During the siege of Paris in 1870–1871, pigeons were used, as well as in both World Wars. During World War I, pigeons were used mainly at night to carry messages. The English-bred "Cher Ami" (Dear Friend) became famous. The bird served with a battalion from New York that was stationed on the front line near Verdun. In spite of loss of a foot and a wound to the head, the bird carried a message on its wounded leg to its home cote — a distance of 25 miles (40 km) in 25 minutes. During World War II at least 32 pigeons received the 1943-inaugurated Dickin Medal for brave service. During this war pigeons were extensively used to carry secret messages to American agents behind enemy lines. In 1956, the American army sold its last pigeons, to make way for computers and other electronic gadgets.

It is not known exactly when the pigeon fancy first started, but the Romans certainly kept lots of pigeons; some towers attached to Roman houses contained over 5,000 birds! Besides the instinct to return to their birthplace, some pigeon breeds have the tendency to acrobatic flight, including tumbling, rolling, and flying around at very high altitudes. Such acrobatic flying is a tendency in all domestic pigeon breeds, but is scarcely seen in the wild rock dove (*Columba livia*). Such talents must have been intensified in the domestic birds through years of selective breeding. After the Romans, the Crusaders must have had a lot to do with the broadening of the pigeon fancy, which had had a long period of popularity in the Far East. As trade increased with Arabia and Persia, many pigeon breeds were brought to Europe over sea or land. In his work *Ornithologia*, published in 1616, the Italian scholar Aldrovandi tells how various breeds of pigeons from Asia were brought to central and western Europe by Dutch and English seafarers. The fancy spread from the ports into the hinterland. Many paintings by the Dutch masters of the 17th century, such as those of Melchior d'Hondecoeter and Adriaan van Utrecht, show illustrations of pigeon varieties then known. Development of communication led to exchange of information about fancy pigeons from various locations. Original breeds were further improved through personal taste. Brothers and sisters were crossed with their parents or with each other to produce local strains.

Toward the end of the 19th century the first bird exhibitions were organized, and pigeons played a major role. To produce uniformity of the various

Domesticated Pigeons

breeds, comprehensive, sometimes unnatural standards were set, whereby ideal markings and colors were produced that sometimes extended the frontiers of genetics. (At that time, Mendel's rules of genetics were not yet fully understood.)

In the meantime, the pigeon fancy has developed over 200 different breeds, in infinite varieties of color and markings, by means of the finest selective breeding principles that will ensure their preservation.

The show season, normally from November through January, is, with the breeding season, the high point of the pigeon fancy. The organization of the first bird shows was the basis for the expansion of the hobby. The shows are now held annually and are of international renown. In Europe, the Federal Republic of Germany and the East German Democratic Republic lead in the exhibition of pigeons. In Belgium, the shows in Ghent and Brussels are well known, and the Dairy Show in Great Britain is unique. In Paris, the pigeon show is combined with that of other animals. The pigeon fancy in France as well as Italy is not up to international standard, but is much better organized in Holland, Scandinavia, Switzerland, Austria, and Czechoslovakia, where enormous shows have first class exhibits. In the United States we are fast achieving European standards. In Australia, South Africa, and New Zealand the pigeon fancy is also recognized as an interesting pastime, although the breeding and show seasons are dependent on climatic factors.

Dovecotes or Pigeon Lofts

Plans of the 9th-century Abbey of St. Gall in France show that a large pigeon cote as well as a large duck pond were contained in the abbey garden. We can surmise that at that time most pigeons were kept to have a year-round meat supply.

The monks kept many kinds of animals and cultivated various edible and medicinal plants. They wrote comprehensive manuscripts detailing their observations and their techniques of management. These documents, which have proven invaluable for posterity, were also of importance to other abbeys.

It is probable that English monks were well into pigeon breeding long before the Norman Conquest. The oldest surviving stone dovecote in England, built about 1100, is the Dove House at Haddenham in Buckinghamshire, while a 540-hole roost cote of similar age is to be found near Duster in Somerset. The interior of the Duster cote is probably original, including a revolving ladder in excellent condition. This was probably used by the owner to examine the nests, to take care of eggs or chicks, or to remove them.

The circular built dovecote at Bemerton, near Salisbury, Wiltshire, Southern England, is also famous. Of special note are cross-shaped glassless windows and the conical roof with an open top that serves as a central source of light and ventilation.

After the 16th-century English Reformation, many dovecotes came into the hands of lay people

Ancient English dovecotes. Top left: Stone dovecote at Bemerton, Wiltshire, near Salisbury; the classic form of a round tower with holes near the eaves. Top right: The 1,000 bird dovecote at Athelhampton, Dorset. Bottom: The Seventeenth-century dovecote at Grassington, in Yorkshire.

Domesticated Pigeons

and were frequently found on large estates, wealthy farms, or in parks. Still intact, the impressive Dove House at Athelhampton, Dorset, can house over 1,000 pigeons. Even more pigeons could be housed in the Tudor dovecote at Willington, close to Bedford. This majestic building, which housed nearly 1,500 pigeons, was erected by Sir John Gostwick, Cardinal Wolsey's Master of Horse.

Catherine of Medici, the wife of Henry II of France, was responsible for many of the numerous dovecotes built in France in the 16th century. The cote on the grounds of Chateau Talcy is well worth a visit. Catherine had it built for her cousin Bernard de Saviate in 1520.

In the meantime, England had not been standing still with regard to dovecotes. By the outbreak of the English Civil War in 1648 there were 26,000 of them according to Samuel Hartlib, who wrote to his friend, poet John Milton: "Pigeons are now a hurtful fowle by reason of their multitude and the number of houses erected daille for their increase."

In Scotland, the pigeon fancy was also not neglected, especially in 1603 as James VI of Scotland took the English crown. Beautiful dovecotes can still be seen; the one at Polmont, close to Falkirk is particularly notable. It was built around 1647; over the main entrance is the coat of arms of its first owner, William Livingstone.

In the 17th century dovecotes were built in even the remotest corners of England. A good example is the square dovecote built in 1600 at Penmon, near Beaumaris in Anglesey, Wales, with a domed vault and hexagonal cupola. During the mid-17th century, English yeoman farmers began to keep pigeons. It is interesting that pigeon lofts were incorporated in the framework of the farmhouse itself. A good example is to be found in a farmhouse just outside Grassington in Yorkshire.

Towards the end of the 17th century, dovecotes became smaller and fanciers began to concentrate on particular breeds. Attractive examples of such cotes can be found in the gardens of Chateau de Villesavin, Loire et Cher, and Tour en Sologne. "Here," writes Sonia Roberts (in: *Bird-keeping and Birdcages*, Drake Publishers, New York, 1973), "the 17th century dovecote is designed to harmonize with the white marble fountains that are the major feature of the grounds. The ultimate switch of the dovecote from use to ornament occurs in the gardens of the Chateau de Canon, which were remodelled in the 18th century for a close friend of Voltaire. These gardens are famous for their chartreuses — squares surrounded by thick, green-clad walls and filled with flowers in the springtime — and are positively littered with toy dovecotes, as well as busts, statues, and miniature temples, both classical and Chinese in style."

In the 18th and 19th centuries, interest in the pigeon fancy remained stable, but increased in the 1920s, when many old dovecotes were restored and populated with various breeds. Splendid Tudor dovecotes can be admired in Nymans, Sussex; Chastleton and Rousham House, Oxfordshire; Bingham's Melcombe, Dorset; Eardisland and Old Sufton, Herefordshire; Wynyates, Warwickshire; Quenington Nauton and Daglingworth, Gloucestershire; Charleston Manor, Sussex; and Fyfield in Wilts.

Considerations Before Purchase

Are Pigeons Right for You?

Before obtaining any pigeons, carefully consider the following points:
• Why do you want to keep pigeons? Is it for your own enjoyment or are there other factors that have aroused your interest?
• Are the other members of the family receptive to your plans?
• Are you able to afford the expense? (It is not only the pigeons themselves that can be costly; consider also the cost of building a cote, the daily food, and the occasional services of an avian veterinarian.)
• Do you want to keep and breed pigeons for exhibition and competition? Are you knowledgeable enough to enter such competitions? Can you handle the disappointment of failing to win a prize?
• Do you want to concentrate on a certain breed, or would you prefer to have a variety of breeds?
• Do you have room to keep pigeons (spacious house, large garden)? If you want to keep free-flying pigeons, will your neighbors accept seeing your birds in *their* gardens and on *their* roofs? Damage caused by your pigeons may not be confined to your own property but may also affect your neighbors. And remember that no one will be pleased to find droppings on their patios! (It might be wise to share your plans with your neighbors and discuss possible drawbacks—as well as possible enjoyment. It is better to have cooperation at the outset than to have problems later.)
• Last, but not least, do you have adequate time each day to care for your birds? When you return home from work, you will have to feed and water your birds and clean out the cote. Can you still do this after the first enthusiasm has passed? Have you thought about how you can arrange care for your birds while you are on vacation?

Never lightly take up a hobby such as pigeon keeping. Think carefully about all aspects of the commitment and discuss them with every member of your family. Taking care of an animal is a full time job, not to be taken lightly.

Pigeons and Other House Pets

Dogs: Pigeons usually soon get used to a dog, but not every dog remains peaceful towards pigeons. Hunting dogs in particular, however well they may have been trained, will be most unreliable towards your pigeons. The natural hunting instinct will occasionally take the upper hand and can result in a massacre of your free-flying pigeons. Moreover, barking and overactive dogs may result in the pigeons' not leaving the cote or spending too much time in your neighbor's garden or on your neighbor's roof.

Cats: Experience has shown that cats are "no-nos" in a house or garden where birds are kept. Sooner or later, pigeons will be killed by cats. Free-flying pigeons also attract wild birds to the garden and you do not want to put these in danger from a prowling cat.

Guinea Pigs and Rabbits: These animals and pigeons will pose no danger to each other. If you have guinea pigs and rabbits in outdoor pens, however, the free-flying pigeons will appropriate their pellet food.

Planning for Your Vacation

As mentioned, it is essential to have knowledgeable friends or acquaintances who can care for your birds when you and your family are on vacation. The necessity of membership in a local pigeon club will make itself clear in this case! Neighbors or friends with no knowledge of pigeons will not be

Above right: The carrier or English carrier. As early as 1700 the birds were used to transport letters from one place to another. In the USA they were exhibited in 1873.
Above left: The barb one of the oldest breeds known was mentioned in Shakespeare's play "As You Like It" (1600)
Below left: The Steinheimer Bagdad is originally from Germany, and has a somewhat curved beak.
Below right: The dragon is originally from England.

Considerations Before Purchase

aware of the responsibility of the task. Whoever is to care for your birds while you are away should first visit on several occasions to learn how your operation works. Go together through a "dress rehearsal"! It can help for your pigeons to observe the "normal boss" and the "temporary boss" together; the birds will then be less confused than if a caring but complete stranger suddenly shows up and starts doing the chores.

If you have no club colleague to help, it is possible to enlist the help of an "amateur." Give as much instruction as possible, with a list of the things to do each day. Be sure to have an adequate supply of food, grit, etc.; it would be unfair for your friend to have to do the shopping as well!

Give your helper your vacation address and, in particular, phone numbers at which you can be reached in any emergency. If you are concerned, you can also phone your friend while you are away to advise about special problems that may arise. The telephone number of your veterinarian should also be left with your helper.

Above: The frillback's place of origin is believed to be Asia Minor.
Below: The gentle and beautiful fantails are thought to have come from India. This breed "is one of the daintiest of birds. It gives the impression of a Dresden doll, with a background of starched ruffles of lace or paper." (W. M. Levi)

Purchasing Pigeons

Where to Get Pigeons

Without question, the best place to purchase pigeons is from local club members or from a reputable dealer.

The show season is a particularly good time to purchase new stock. If you are a novice in the hobby, enlist the help of an experienced fancier when going to see prospective purchases. Discuss the birds with their owners and ask what prizes the birds have won in shows. It does not require much effort to find out the quality of a breeder. An outstanding breeder will most likely have good stock for sale.

Advertisements for many pigeon breeds may also be found in the various magazines and journals (see page 77). In these ads, numbers may be used before the birds in question. The code for sexes is as follows:

1–2 as prefix means: 1 male, 2 females

1–0 means: 1 male

0–1 means: 1 female

1–1 means: 1 male and 1 female, or 1 pair.

How to Recognize Healthy Pigeons

Genuine pigeon fanciers should never buy inferior stock. Here is how to recognize a healthy bird:
• The plumage (with the exception of certain breeds such as Frillbacks and Owls) should be glossy and full.
• The color of the plumage must be bright and clean; dull-colored feathering indicates bad health.
• A pigeon's eyes must be bright and alert. A pigeon's eye color shows a distinct correlation with the color of its head. In general, a pigeon with white head plumage will have dark colored eyes, while a pigeon with colored head plumage will have reddish or yellowish eyes. There are, however, some breeds in which the opposite prevails (Moorheads,

for example). The more fiery the eyes, the greater amount of pigment they contain. This strong pigment is also contained in the plumage, and this can be seen on the surface of the feathers as a gloss. The yellow pigment is missing on the surface of dark-colored eyes, therefore all you see are the blood vessels. This absence of pigment on the eye surface is related to the absence of pigment in the feathers around the eye. This can often be seen in the white, eye-ring feathers of the Moorhead.
• A pigeon's droppings should be relatively firm and well formed. The feathers around the vent should be dry and clean and not smeary.
• Healthy fancy pigeons are active and curious. They should not become excited when taken into the owner's hand for examination.
• Healthy fancy pigeons are not infested with ectoparasites (mites, fleas, or ticks). Infested birds have white, scaly deposits on the eyelids, beak corners, legs, toes, and/or around the vent, are restless, and/or scratch and feather pick themselves severely. Their skin is irritated and their feathers have a "moth-eaten" appearance.

Choice of Breed

Hardy breeds are ideal as free-fliers. My preference includes Old Dutch Capuchines, Old Dutch owls, all varieties of tumblers and high-fliers, all

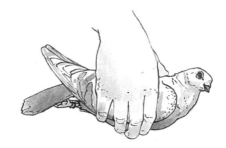

The correct way to hold a pigeon

varieties of color pigeons (ice pigeon, Lahores, Moorheads, etc.), and many cropper varieties. All these varieties will thrill their owner with their frequent flying acrobatics. Young fancy pigeons especially enjoy their free flight, and although such a lifestyle is good for their bodily development, freedom also has its dangers (cats, beasts of prey, birds of prey, etc.) to which they must accustom themselves. Experience has shown that pigeons kept in aviaries and then suddenly allowed free flight will quickly fall prey to predators, since they are used to being protected by wire and glass.

Orientation

Getting pigeons, especially older birds, to be comfortable in new surroundings is problematic. If you obtain new birds in the fall, they will be naturally calm, and if not too lively a breed they can be allowed to fly free after two or three weeks (not earlier!). Before the start of the breeding season pigeons may also be habituated to new surroundings fairly easily; it is more difficult when the birds have formed pairs and are used to a particular breeding cote.

In the mornings, when the birds are first let out, the "old" inhabitants should be released first; then release the newcomers. Be careful not to frighten the new birds so that they fly too far away. If the cote is difficult to see or find, it can be risky to let new birds out, as they will not easily be able to find their way back, even if the older ones find their way back instinctively. It is best therefore to have the cote situated where all the birds can find their way home easily.

Once the new birds fly in and out of the cote, the fancier can relax somewhat. As dusk approaches, many fanciers tap a metal dish filled with seed to attract the birds in. This technique is invariably effective. The birds fly home quickly and greedily eat the offered food. The rule is to feed the birds

only a little before they fly out but to give them adequate food once they fly in to roost for the night.

Transporting Pigeons

Make it a rule never to acquire birds during the winter months, especially if you cannot collect them yourself and they have to travel by public transport. If you are a member of a pigeon club, your club probably owns traveling boxes that you can use for carrying your birds. Even a commercial dog or cat carrier could be used. Several thicknesses of newspaper should be placed on the floor of the carrying container, and over this an ample layer of mini corn-cob bedding or pine shavings, so that all moisture from droppings is absorbed. The container must have openings to supply enough air. If you collect pigeons yourself in a car beware of drafts. Control the airflow by opening a window and starting a slow drive with the ventilation on. Never place the container on a section of the floor that is heated; overheating in the carrying container can cause cardiovascular collapse.

If you have a long journey to make, especially during warm weather, make regular stops, every

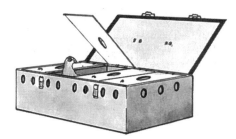

Transport box. The container must have openings to supply enough air for breathing.

$1\frac{1}{2}$–2 hours. Let the birds drink some tepid water or camomile tea (which you will have brought in your thermos).

Housing

One of the first questions once you have decided to keep pigeons is, "How are they best accommodated?" Whether you want to breed and exhibit pigeons or just keep a few birds in an aviary for decoration, the accommodation must be adequate.

Should you want to keep pigeons just for the pleasure of observing them, and now and again to see young in the nest, a simple wall cote will be adequate.

The cote can be built against a wall of the house or garage, preferably a wall that faces south or southwest, in order to get as much sunlight and as little rain as possible.

A wall dovecote.

The size of the cote will depend on the variety of pigeons you intend to keep. It is difficult to choose from the 200 or so named breeds! At first, choose a variety without leg feathers. Avoid varieties that have enormous foot feathering, or those that have extreme shapes. These are more suited to the specialist breeder with appropriate housing. Two breeds come immediately to mind: the Old Dutch owl and the Old Dutch capuchine, respectively an owl and a structure (or form) variety. (See pages 73 and 66). They have a very trusting nature, are easy to keep, and are lovely to look at. In addition, the birds without leg feathers possess a beautiful sheen, but tend to be relatively shy. Tumblers and highfliers can also be recommended.

The Wall Cote

For a medium-sized variety, a cote 26 inches (67 cm) wide, 18 to 20 inches (46–51 cm) deep and 16 inches (41 cm) high is adequate for a pair. A landing board about 8 inches (20 cm) wide, which will also serve as a feeding platform, should be placed along the full length of the cote. While the birds are becoming accustomed to their cote, a mesh cover can be placed over the front. This can be removed when the birds are familiar with their accommodation (see page 20). The mesh can also be used to shut the birds in, which can be necessary in bad weather.

The entrance door, which is 5 × 6 inches (13 × 15 cm) high, may be placed in front, either to the left or to the right.

The cote may be built with the number of compartments to fill your birds' needs. Bear in mind that, after breeding, the new generation of birds will require their own compartments when they become independent. When the young pigeons are old enough to fend for themselves they will be driven from the compartment by their parents. It is advisable to keep spare compartments closed so they are not used indiscriminately by all the pigeons, otherwise new youngsters will not be allowed to use them later.

Various materials may be used to build a cote, but weatherproof triplex or multiplex plywood is probably the best choice, especially for the floor. Although good quality plywood is not likely to rot very quickly, a couple of coats of clear, exterior varnish will assure extra protection against the weather. Nonpoisonous (lead-free) paint may also be used but, unlike clear varnish, it will hide the attractive grain of the wood. Although not absolutely necessary, the interior can also be painted with varnish. It is best to paint the inside of the compartments with a darker color, as pigeons like to breed in as dark an area as possible. Painting the interior with a good waterproof varnish or paint makes it much easier to wash the compartments with warm water when they are soiled.

At one time it was thought that if the inside walls were painted white, this would deter vermin, but this is not true. White walls soon look unclean and require more regular maintenance.

The inner furnishings should be kept as simple as possible. There should be room for two nest bowls in each compartment, in case new eggs are laid before the first brood is independent. It is best to set the second nest bowl on a couple of bricks, so that when the young from the first brood start walking about they do not damage the new eggs.

A covered water drinker and food containers can be constructed and placed on the 8 inches (20 cm) wide landing platform. This can be 7½ inches (19 cm) long, 5 inches (13 cm) wide and 6 inches (15 cm) high. This will prevent fouling of food and water and the edges of the box will be used for perching. A similar box for grit can be placed at the other end of the landing platform.

These covered food containers can never be soiled, even when a bird perches on them.

It must be possible to open, remove, or take apart the front of the cote, with the entrances. This can be done by using hinges or sliding brackets.

If it is not feasible to place the cote so that the front faces other than a westerly or northwesterly direction, it is best to have the inner floor raised 1 inch (2½ cm) above the landing platform, to stop rainwater from running in. The roof may be water-proofed with tarred roofing felt or other suitable roofing material. The uppermost compartment should have a ceiling, so that it is insulated from the roof and is not overheated inside from the sun's rays.

The Pole Cote

A dovecote placed on a pole may look nice in the garden but it is not really suitable for keeping pigeons. It will be exposed to damp and drafts, two dangerous enemies of pigeons. Such a construction is also limited in size, and the compartments would not be deep enough to provide the pigeons with adequate water. In addition, the entrance holes would face all directions, so that half the pigeons would always be exposed to wind and rain. In short, a pole cote is not decent housing for pigeons.

The Garden Cote or Aviary

If you have a garden and you want to take up the hobby of pigeon keeping seriously, perhaps breed-ing various breeds for showing, you are fortunate to be able to fulfill the first consideration of suitable accommodation. If you have a sunny garden, all the better. Pigeons are "sun worshippers" and need the sun's rays to keep them in good health.

Follow the same rules as for the wall cote. The pigeon house should face south or southeast if possible, to avoid direct rain and to allow plenty of sunshine. The size of the aviary will, of course, depend on the amount of available space you have and the number of birds you wish to keep.

A good guideline is to allow 35 cubic feet (1m³) of space for each pair of pigeons, in other words a building approximately 6½ feet (2 m) wide, 8 feet

Housing

(2.5 m) deep, and 6 feet (1.8 m) high, with a volume of approximately 9 cubic meters. Such accommodation is adequate to keep nine pairs of pigeons in good health.

A good pigeon house must be absolutely protected from damp and drafts. Pigeons can withstand heat and extreme cold, but they cannot stand damp and drafts. Another critical standard is ventilation. Because of their rapid respiration and high metabolic rate, pigeons need plenty of oxygen-containing fresh air. In the damp, inclement fall and winter, when the pigeons are closed up in their house, it is easy for an oxygen shortage to occur if ventilation is poor. This must be borne in mind when building the garden cote.

A pigeon garden cote is normally constructed from timber. Stone or bricks may also be used, but give a cold impression. If they must be used, it is best to line the inside wall with timber.

A pigeon garden cote may be built free-standing or against the wall of the house, the garage, or shed. There may be fewer size restrictions for a free-standing cote, but building against a wall also has advantages. You have a good base on which to build and, of course, you will have one wall less to construct.

To keep the building dry, it is recommended that it be constructed at least 16 to 20 inches (41–51 cm) from the ground. This can be accomplished by first laying a concrete foundation about 4 inches (10 cm) thick and then building a 12 to 16 inch (31–41 cm) wall with bricks or concrete blocks around it. Instead of concrete and bricks, you could make a wall of tiles (12 × 12 inches; 31 × 31 cm) placed on top of each other to a height of 16 inches (41 cm) and built to the dimensions of the planned aviary. Timber floor supports, about 2 × 3 inches (5 × 8 cm) are placed on top of the foundation wall at intervals of 20 to 24 inches (51–61 cm). The floor itself can be made from floorboards or ½ inch (12 mm) exterior plywood. Floorboards have the disadvantage that, after time and wear, they tend to warp and separate, making cleaning the floor difficult. You can surmount this problem by lining the floor with ⅛-inch exterior ply. You will then have a smooth, level floor that will be easy to keep clean.

The garden cote or aviary.

Housing

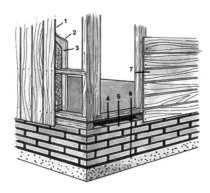

Parts of building.
1. Tongue and groove boards
2. Plywood
3. Insulation
4. Floor of waterproof plywood
5. Bricks
6. Concrete
7. Part of wooden wall

Plants For Your Aviary

("juv." indicates that only young specimens are suitable)

All Huckleberries, Bilberries and relatives
(*Gaylussacidae, Vaccinium*)
American Beech (*Fagus grandifolia*)—juv.
American Holly (*Ilex opaca*)
Arizona Cypress (*Cupressus arizonica*)—juv.
Australian Pine (*Pinus nigra*)—juv.
Balsam Fir (*Abies balsamea*)—juv.
Black Spruce (*Picea mariana*)—juv.
Black Willow (*Salix nigra*)—juv.
Bladdernut (*Staphylea trifolia*)
Chinese or Oriental Cedar (*Thuja orientalis*)
Common Elderberry (*Sambucus nigra*)
Common Juniper (*Juniperus communis*)
Common Privet (*Ligustrum vulgare*)
Coralberry (*Symphoricarpo orbiculatus*)
Douglas Fir (*Pseudotsuga menziesii*)—juv.
Drooping Juniper (*Juniperus flaccida*)
Eastern Hemlock (*Tsuga canadensis*)—juv.
Eastern White Pine (*Pinus strobus*)—juv.

English Holly (*Ilex aquifolium*)
English Ivy (*Hedera helix*)
European Beech (*Fagus sylvatica*)—juv.
European Elderberry (*Sambucus nigra*)
Firethorn (*Cotoneaster pyracantha*)
Hawthorn species (*Crataegus*)—juv.
Mock Orange species (*Philadelphus*)
Multiflora Rose (*Rosa multiflora*)
Northern White Cedar (*Thuja occidentalis*)
Norway Spruce (*Picea abies*)—juv.
Pacific Willow (*Salix lasiandra*)—juv.
Peachleaf Willow (*Salix amyglailoides*)—juv.
Ponderosa Pine (*Pinus ponderosa*)—juv.
Prunus species
Raspberries (*Rubus*)
Red Elderberry (*Sambucus racemosa pubens*)
Red Spruce (*Picea rubens*)—juv.
Rocky Mountain Juniper (*Juniperus scopolorum*)
Scotch Pine (*Pinus sylvestris*)—juv.
Snowberry (*Symphoricarpos albus*)
Subalpine Fir (*Abies lasiocarpa*)—juv.
Spirea species (*Sorbaria*)
Spruce Pine (*Pinus glabra*)—juv.
Tamarack (*Larix laricina*)—juv.
Viburnum species
Virginia Pine (*Pinus virginiana*)—juv.
Western White Pine (*Pinus monticola*)—juv.
Whin (*Genista tinctoria*)
White Fir (*Abies concolor*)—juv.
White Poplar (*Populus alba*)—juv.
White Spruce (*Picea glauca*)—juv.

Flooring, Walls, and Roofing

It is best not to use slippery floor coverings, especially if you intend to keep some of the long-legged varieties of pigeons. Although ½ inch (12 mm) exterior ply is expensive, it is perhaps the best type of flooring for a pigeon aviary; if it is well varnished or painted it will be easy to keep clean and will last for years.

The walls are built up from the edges of the floor. Scrap wood may be used for the framework; cover this with shiplap or tongue-and-groove boarding. It is best to have the framework flush with the edge of the floor; the boards can overlap the foundation to keep out the rain.

Before covering the framework, the corner poles should be bolted together with long bolts and nuts. It is easy to make a double-walled aviary by lining the inside of the framework with plywood. Between the inner and outer walls, insulation (such as glass fiber) can be used. This will help keep out cold weather and ensure a more constant interior temperature.

The roof may be made in a choice of styles. The best is a double-pitched roof covered with tiles or slates, but other designs can also be used. It is really a matter of taste. A double-pitched roof is made from triangular roof trusses (made with timber battens). These are fixed to the walls and joined together with battens, to which the tiles are fixed. A pitched roof can also be made from solid timber and covered with roofing felt. It is a good idea to suspend the ridge a little above the roof to allow for good through ventilation. If the cote is built against a wall, to make it watertight, flashing must be used between the wall and the sloping roof, about 4 to 6 inches (10–15 cm) higher at the back. If the front wall is 6 feet (2 m) high the back wall should be at least 3 inches (8 cm) higher; this way, the nest boxes can be placed higher at the back, leaving plenty of space beneath them. It is recommended that openings for ventilation be left under the front of the roof. Whether a single-pitched or double-pitched roof is used, it is advisable to install a lightweight ceiling.

Nest Compartments

The size and number of compartments in the pigeon aviary will depend on the type of pigeons to be kept. If you intend to keep varieties that can reliably rear their own young (which is the case with most long-beaked and medium-beaked breeds), two compartments will be adequate. If you intend to keep varieties that cannot rear their own young, have a minimum of three compartments. With a two-compartment house, one compartment can be used for breeding, the other for young pigeons during the breeding season. When the sexes are separated in the winter, the cocks can be left in the breeding compartment, while the hens can be placed with any recently arrived youngsters in the other compartment.

Although roominess is recommended, it is best not to make individual compartments too large, as they will be more drafty. It is much better to have three compartments 6½ feet (2 m) wide than one compartment 19½ feet (6 m) wide.

Pigeons kept in large spaces can become evasive and shy. In smaller spaces they cannot shy away and soon become much tamer. The smaller compartments are especially useful for pigeons such as highfliers and tumblers. In addition, a smaller compartment is easier to service. The height of the house should not be more than 72 to 76 inches (185–195 cm). If the house is much higher, the pigeon will be able to fly above the breeder's head, which is undesirable if the birds are to become tame.

The depth of the aviary can be about 8 feet (2.5 m). If nest boxes of 20 inches (51 cm) depth are placed against the rear wall, this will leave 6½ feet (2 m) of working space. As we have already discussed, an aviary that is 6½ feet (2 m) wide, 8 feet (2.5 m) deep, and 5 feet 9 inches (1.8 m) high is adequate for nine pairs of pigeons. In this case, nine individual breeding compartments must be provided for the birds.

The best size for medium-sized varieties such as Old Dutch owls and Old Dutch capuchines is 25½ inches (65 cm) wide, 20 inches (5 cm) deep, and 16 inches (41 cm) high. This may seem a little large, but is just right for confining a new pair of birds together. In addition, the width is required for two nesting pans.

The rear wall is 6½ feet (2 m) long and 5 feet 9 inches (1.8 m) high; nine breeding compartments of the size given will fit precisely if three rows of three are made and, if we place the boxes as high as possible, this will leave a space of 21 inches (54 cm) below the bottom row. This space can be used for the grit and food containers and the water drinkers.

The front of the nesting compartments may be completely open, slightly open, or half open. It is best to be able to remove or replace the fronts.

Front view of breeding compartments.

The advantage of having wholly open or half-open compartments is that if a strange cock gets into the compartment, it will be easier for the "rightful owner" to drive him out. On the other hand, a strange bird may not be able to enter a slightly open-fronted compartment so easily, but if he does get in he cannot be driven out so easily. The fronts may be hinged or simply affixed with a couple of screws.

The front may be made from square weld mesh or from vertical wooden doweling. Dowel has the advantage that less dirt and fewer feathers adhere to it. It is most convenient to have the floor of the compartments flat and level with the front. This way the droppings can easily be cleaned out with a triangular scraper. The floor is best made from exterior ply, but you can also use ⅛-inch exterior ply over floorboards. Chipboard should not be used; if wet this can give off toxic fumes that are unhealthy for both pigeons and humans.

The nesting compartments for larger varieties, such as Dutch croppers, German muffed magpie croppers, and English pouters, must be somewhat larger. These birds must be trained for exhibition, so it is recommended that the compartments be built to double as training cages during the show season. Show cages are usually 20 × 20 × 20 inches (51 × 51 × 51 cm), and this is a good size for the nesting compartments. Four such compartments can be made on our 6½ feet × 5 feet 9 inches (2 × 1.8 m) high wall. These may be 20 inches (51 cm) wide and 20 inches (51 cm) deep; we need to diminish the height a little.

The compartments, each 18 inches (46 cm) high, may be placed in three rows one above another, this leaving a space beneath of 15 inches (38 cm). Horizontally, four compartments 39½ × 20 inches (100 × 51 cm). Three such rows will give space for six breeding pairs.

After the breeding season, the slides can be placed in the double compartments to make each one into two training cages.

A similar system may be used for the popular dwarf cropper varieties, such as the English pygmy pouters, Bruenner croppers, and Holle croppers. These varieties require a training cage with dimensions of 16 × 16 × 16 inches (41 × 41 × 41 cm), and this can also be the basis for the breeding compartments. On a back wall of 6½ feet (2 m) length, this does not work out quite so well, as there would be one odd cage. However, one can make the back wall 7 feet 2 inches (2.2 m) in length, allowing enough room for six compartments, which can be separated into three during the breeding season.

Doors and Windows

Doors must be installed in the compartment dividing walls; these may be 26 inches (67 cm) wide and 64½ inches (165 cm) high, or as high as the dividing wall. The bottom of the door should be made of solid hardboard or plywood, so that the sexes cannot get too close to each other when they are kept separated. The upper part of the door can be made from weld mesh or doweling. A hinged door is better than a sliding door. A sliding door takes too much wall space that could be used for perching facilities.

The front window of the aviary can be made from floor to ceiling, or perhaps 20 inches (51 cm) from the floor. In short, great variety is possible. Large windows give the aviary a look of roominess and a free view; glass, however, is a good conductor of heat, so large glass areas will cause great temperature fluctuations in the aviary. In autumn especially, there can be a great range of temperature between day and night. Small windows minimize the problem, but they do not let in much light.

If the front of the aviary is 6½ × 5 feet 9 inches (2 × 1.8 m), the window can be 4 feet 7 inches (1.4 m) long and 3 feet 7 inches (1.1 m) high. The bottom

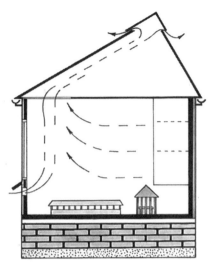

Ventilation of a peaked roof

ventilator slide can be opened to allow fresh air into the cote. The air escapes via the ceiling through the roof.

The Outdoor Run

We must ensure that pigeons are allowed to enjoy ample fresh air and sunlight. The best way to do this is to construct an outdoor run from 2 × 2 inch (5×5 cm) lumber; the length and height of the aviary by 5 feet (1.5 m) deep is adequate, but the deeper the better. The timber frame is covered with a fairly fine mesh. This can be green, plastic-covered mesh, or square-holed welded mesh of the type used by aviculturists. One drawback of the plastic-covered mesh is that it can be difficult to see through it; however, it is very strong and will last a long time. Galvanized mesh rusts after a few years and must be replaced. On no account must wide-gauge mesh be used; mice will gain entry to the aviary. These little pests can consume and spoil a large proportion of the pigeons' food and, of course, can carry infectious diseases to your stock.

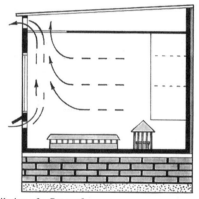

Ventilation of a flat roof

of the window will then be 20 inches (51 cm) above the floor. With this recommendation, the inside of the pigeon house will receive adequate daylight, and temperatures will remain within the required range. The window can be divided into two and can be sash or sliding style.

Just under the window, a ventilating panel 16 inches (41 cm) long and 4 inches (10 cm) high can be installed. This is controlled by a slide which can be fully closed, fully opened, or partly opened to allow the appropriate amount of ventilation at any given time. When the windows are closed, the

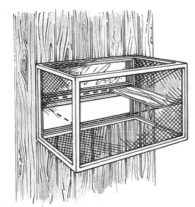

A window run with a wire bottom.

Pigeon perches and single nests

Another kind of run or flight is one that is raised from the ground and built out from a window. The framework, including the bottom, is covered with ½-inch mesh. It should be deep enough to allow the window to be opened 90°.

The floor of the outside run can consist of clean sand and/or garden earth planted with grass. Various weedseeds can be sown now and again; as the little seedlings grow, they will be greedily eaten by the birds.

Clean sand is more hygienic, but garden earth and grass are more natural. The latter is certainly more likely to be appreciated by the pigeons.

A pigeon likes to have a quiet spot where it can remain undisturbed. It is therefore necessary to install numerous boxes and perches. The so-called "saddle" or V-shaped perch is easy to make; it can also be purchased. Some models are made of plastic. The perches should be attached at least 14 inches (36 cm) from the wall; there must also be at least 14 inches (36 cm) difference in height between two perches.

Box perches are the simplest and take up little space. Each box measures 10×10×4 inches (26×26 × 10 cm) deep. Sixteen such boxes can be constructed in a space of about 10 square feet (1 sq m), whereas only six saddle perches could be installed in the same space. For medium-sized or large pigeon varieties, the boxes should be 12 × 12 inches (31 × 31 cm), with the same depth of 4 inches (10 cm). Perches for feather-footed varieties should be of a totally different pattern. The foot feathers must be protected from damage. The perch must be fashioned so that the birds can turn without their foot feathers coming into contact with the walls or other objects. The best for these are wooden discs about 4 inches (10 cm) in diameter, and mounted onto metal brackets that bring them out from the wall about 16 to 20 inches (41–51 cm), depending on the size of the breed.

It is best not to have too many perches in the outside flight. These will be used by only two or three dominant cocks who will drive the other inmates away.

Food and Water Containers

The aviary must be further furnished with containers for food, water, and grit. The best type is the feeding trough. Various types are commercially available, but you can easily make a trough yourself. The trough can be made from formica, with a width of 4½ inches (11.5 cm) and a height of 2 inches (5 cm). Each pigeon requires about 5 inches (13 cm) of length, so if we have 18 pigeons, for example, the two-sided trough should be at least 45 inches (1.2 m) long. For stability, an end plate,

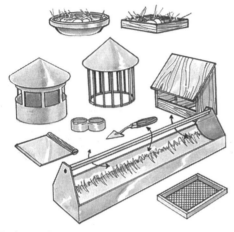

Equipment for pigeons. From top to bottom: Nest pans, seed or water container, grit or water pan cover, grit hopper, seed cups, scrapers, feeder, sieve.

consisting of a piece of plank 6 inches (15–16 cm) wide is glued to each end of the trough. This plate is only 1 inch (3 cm) wide at the top and 5 inches (13 cm) high. Above the trough, a 1 inch (3 cm) diameter piece of dowel is fixed, or a roof can be fixed over it.

Drinking containers are available in various shapes. The best type is the enamel or porcelain water fountain, especially the former. Plastic containers are not as good, especially in the summer when the water becomes too warm. To prevent dirt and feathers from entering the water, the fountain should be placed on a shelf 16 to 20 inches (41–51 cm) above the floor. To complete the furnishings there should be a grit container.

The Roof Cote

A cote constructed in the attic has the advantage of being bone-dry and usually draft-free. Disadvantages are that attics are commonly dark and difficult to ventilate. But these problems can be overcome; there are many excellent and interesting examples of roof cotes in various towns. You can make a flight outside a dormer window, but you may need permission under local building codes. Basic construction rules are the same as for the garden aviary. To let more light into the cote, you can replace some of the roof tiles with glass tiles. A sliding window is better, in that it is more difficult to break than a hinged one. The outside run should have a solid floor. The furnishings are the same as those de-

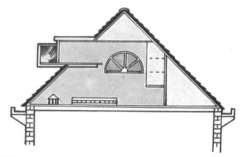

The attic or roof cote.

scribed for the garden cote, but we must take the sloping walls into consideration. If the loft is spacious enough, it is best to build vertical walls inside it. A ceiling and ventilators are essential.

Single-Pair Cote

Another possibility is to build a single-pair cote. A cote for a single pair of pigeons is really an enlarged individual nesting compartment, in which the pigeons are permanently contained. There are advantages and disadvantages. One great advantage is that the pair of pigeons are not disturbed by other birds in the breeding season, which would be the case in a community cote. Also, breeders who

A single-pair cote

are allergic to the dust of pigeon droppings in the large cote will have fewer problems if the birds are kept in single-pair cotes.

A disadvantage is that you require a lot more room if you wish to keep a large number of birds. Another disadvantage is that the birds have minimum freedom of movement; a partial remedy is to make the cote as large as possible. It is best to build a small flight in front of the cote, so that the birds can be let out for exercise. The flight can also be used to shut the birds out when you are cleaning the cote.

For small to medium–sized varieties, a single cote should have minimum dimensions of 47 inches (120 cm) long, 23½ to 28 inches (60–72 cm) deep and 22 to 23½ inches (56–60 cm) high. The depth of the cote depends on availible space and the wind direction. If the front of the cote faces south or southeast, then 23½ inches (60 cm) is adequate; if the front faces in any other direction it must be

deeper to provide greater protection from the weather. The height of 22 to 23½ inches (56–60 cm) is necessary so that a 10– to 12–inch (26–31 cm) wide shelf for a second nest container can be placed about half way up. Further furnishings consist of a sturdy perch and a smaller shelf of 4 inches (10 cm) wide, fixed 8 inches (20 cm) above the floor, to protect the food, water, and grit containers.

It is recommended (if you have no safety flight), to have a dividing slide in the cote, so that the birds

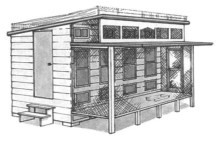

A homing pigeon cote.

cannot escape during cleaning operations.

In this chapter, we have examined a number of possibilities for housing pigeons. There are many other kinds of housing, but here are adequate basic principles for the prospective pigeon keeper to make a start in housing birds.

If you are unable to build your own cote, you can buy one ready made. In "small animal" literature, excellent pigeon cotes are often advertised. Even homing pigeon cotes are ideal for pigeons. These cotes can be obtained in many sizes, with double or single walls, while windows can be made to measure. The roof can be double-pitched, with slate or tiles. In short, there are many possibilities.

Suitable Food and Proper Feeding

The rock pigeon (*Columba livia*), along with a large number of other bird species, is herbivorous. Also called seedeaters, these birds must obtain all their essential nutrients from various kinds of ripe and unripe seeds, cereals, and legumes. These nutrients must provide warmth and energy, and support various physiological and reproductive functions, such as replacement of plumage and the production of eggs.

Carbohydrates and Fats

In relation to their volume, pigeons have a large surface area. To maintain their high body temperature of 107.2°F (41.8°C), they require an enormous amount of energy. This, of course, must come from the diet. The two constituents of the diet that produce energy and heat are carbohydrates and fats. Seeds, cereals, and legumes contain from 40–75% carbohydrates. Fats are sparse in cereals and legumes, but several seeds are fairly rich in fat.

Carbohydrates consist of sugars and starches. They are broken down in the body to form soluble sugars, which are converted to glycogen for storage in the liver. From here it goes as needed to the muscles, where the glucose is used as fuel to produce energy and heat as a by-product. Fats produce 2¼ times as much energy as carbohydrates; since our captive fancy pigeons do not use as much energy as they would in the wild, fats are not so necessary. Fats not burned up by activity will become deposited in the pigeon's muscles and body organs, making it obese and unhealthy. The bird will become lethargic and lazy, its reproductive drive will be reduced, and egg production will fall. A low-fat diet is therefore recommended; more about this subject later in the text.

Protein

A pigeon's body is composed of millions of cells, each of which is formed mainly from proteins. Countless cells die off regularly, and these must be replaced. Proteins are necessary in the diet for the growth, replacement, and repair of cell tissues. Proteins consist of amino acids, which could be called the building bricks of proteins. There are about 24 different kinds of amino acids, but they are not all contained in a single protein. However three or more combinations are contained in various legumes, cereals, and seeds. For example, the garden pea contains an amino acid combination of 1, 8, and 17; wheat, a combination of 6, 10, and 21. Another important function of proteins is the production of enzymes to aid in the digestive system. A large proportion of proteins is obtained from legumes (about 16–23%), but also in cereals (around 11%). However, the amino acid compositions are different in the various legumes and cereals, so a mixture must be provided in order to ensure a balanced diet. The plumage is also composed mainly from proteins and a good supply of these nutrients is necessary before and during the annual molt in the fall.

For some time before and during the breeding season a wide variety of proteins is essential for egg production. The so-called pigeon's "milk," which is produced from the crop lining, must be as rich in protein as possible. It is probable that the protein hormone prolactin is responsible for the production of this secretion. Pigeons that do not receive a varied supply of amino acids will not be able to provide an adequate diet to their young through the crop milk.

The vegetable proteins supplied to our pigeons are not altogether adequate. Certain essential amino acids are contained only in animal proteins. Research has shown that wild pigeons regularly take animal food such as small snails, slugs, and various insects, and these are necessary to provide a full complement of amino acids and a balanced diet. We must therefore take this into consideration when feeding our pigeons that are confined to cages and lofts; remember that they are barely able to find adequate animal food in captive conditions. More on this later.

Suitable Food and Proper Feeding

Minerals

Mineral salts are a very important ingredient of a pigeon's diet. Although not strictly classed as food, minerals are an essential supplement. They are inorganic materials that play an important role in the structure of the skeleton, in growth, and in body functions. The eggshell is composed largely from minerals. Minerals are categorized into macroelements and microelements. Macroelements are those of which a relatively large quantity is required (such as calcium and phosphorous) while microelements, or trace elements, are those required only in minute quantities.

Together with vitamin D3, calcium and phosphorus play an essential role in the forming and maintenance of the bones. These minerals are not contained in sufficient quantities in the normal diet, so must be given in the form of grit. Good quality mineral grit may be purchased from your local pet store or feed supplier.

Vitamins

Vitamins, which are found in foodstuffs in very small quantities, are complicated organic compounds of animal or vegetable origin. They are necessary for the maintenance and renewal of body cells and for the efficient functioning of the organs. Most vitamins cannot be manufactured in the body, but are obtained in small but sufficient quantities from today's balanced diet. In some cases, however, vitamin supplements may be beneficial (see page 30).

Water

Finally, we come to water, the elixir of life. Water is necessary to lubricate and soften the food, to regulate body temperature, and to serve as a transport system for digested food. Therefore, pigeons should have free access to fresh, clean water at all times (see page 35).

Quality of Ingredients

The cereals, legumes, and seeds we feed our pigeons must be of the highest quality. Food must not smell musty, nor show even a trace of mold. Spoilage results from storage in damp conditions. It is often difficult to judge the quality of cereals and legumes, so they should be obtained only from reliable suppliers.

Grain, seed, and legumes should have a moisture content not greater than 17%. If higher than this the nutritional quality, including the vitamin content, will be diminished. Damp grain can cause digestive problems. Under normal conditions, the moisture content is well under 17%. All ingredients must be kept dry and protected from rodents in a well-ventilated room. Regularly stir the food so that the air can run through it. A good method is to store the food in a silo (hopper) with a tap on the bottom. The advantage of this is that the oldest food is used first; also, each time a portion is drawn off, the remaining food is moved.

Correct feeding is one of the most important factors in keeping a good breeding stud of pigeons. The food must include a great variety of cereals, legumes, and seeds. The pigeon year is divided into seasons, with the appropriate diet for each season. It is advisable to know why some ingredients should be given in larger quantities than others.

Cereals

Cereals are excellent food for pigeons and should not be left out of a food mixture at any time of the year. Grains have a high starch content (40–75%) and are easily digested. The fat content is

Suitable Food and Proper Feeding

low (to 4%). The protein content is not particularly high (to 11%), but provides a good supplement to the legumes.

Barley

Barley is an excellent nutritious food for pigeons. It has a starch content of 62.5%, a protein content of 7.5%, and a low fat content of 1.2%. The fiber (roughage) content is 1.3%. Like other cereals, barley has a high vitamin B content. Unlike most other grains, barley has a good vitamin D and mineral content. During the molting and resting period barley is especially valuable; since it is nutritious but not so greedily consumed, the pigeons will eat moderately but healthfully.

Why is barley not so avidly taken? It cannot be the taste, as groats (dehusked barley) are taken readily. Barley has a prickly extension at the end of the husk that may irritate the tongue and throat of the pigeons. Long, thin barley has a particularly sharp husk, so give your birds the short, fat variety. Even so, pigeons are not great barley fans. Some breeders say simply, "My pigeons will not eat barley." This is nonsense: if a pigeon is hungry it will eat anything, even barley! It is a matter of what you want them to eat. Barley should also be available during the breeding season. Ten percent of the feed mix is adequate, so that the parents do not feed too much to the young. During the molt 20–25% barley in the feed is ideal. Barley is very good for feather condition. After the molt, during the rest season, 50% barley can be given; this stops egg laying and provides a good vitamin D supply, which is essential in the winter.

Maize (Sweet corn)

Maize comes in different varieties, colors, and sizes. For pigeons the small to medium varieties with yellow to orange color are best. These contain the most carotene, a provitamin A that is converted to usable vitamin A in the pigeon's body. White and pale yellow maize contain much less carotene.

Maize has the lowest protein content of the cereals (7.1%), but a high starch content (65.7%), and a fiber content of 1.3%. It has the highest fat content of grains or legumes (4%). Maize is avidly consumed by pigeons and, because of its high fat content, it should be given sparingly (maximum 20% of the diet). In intense cold weather we could increase this to 30% so that the pigeons can compensate for heat loss. Smaller varieties of pigeons can be given crushed maize, which is more easily swallowed.

Wheat

Wheat is an excellent food for pigeons and it is eagerly consumed. Its digestible protein content is somewhat higher than that of other grains: 9.7%; the starch content is 63.5%; fat content, 1.2%; the raw fiber content is low at 0.9%. Wheat must be of good quality and should form a maximum of 20% of the diet. Too much wheat can cause digestive problems.

Oats

Oats are a good food for pigeons. This grain stimulates the nervous system and is particularly useful in preparing for the breeding season. Oats cause the birds to become more active. The drawbacks of oats are a high fat content (4%) and a higher proportion of fiber than other grains (2.6%; double that of barley). Dehusked oats, with no loss of quality, are more acceptable to the birds. Because of the high fat content, oats should not be more than 5% of the diet. The protein content is 9.3% and the starch content 44.8%.

Above left: The white king is of American origin.
Above right: The Cauchois, an ancient French breed.
Center left: The clean-legged, striking Hungarian or *Huhnschecke* is originally from upper Austria.
Center right: The Maltese a so-called fowl or hen pigeon.
Below left: The Polish lynx, developed near Cracow.
Below right: The Strasser is originally from Austria.

Suitable Food and Proper Feeding

Brown Rice (Paddy)

Brown (unmilled) rice is a valuable food because of its high vitamin B content. The vitamin is contained in the husk and in the germ, and is more or less lost in dehusked rice. Brown rice has a fairly high fiber content. Its protein and fat content are lower than in other grains. In proportion to the quantity of fiber, the starch content can also be considered low, but this is compensated for by the vitamin B content. An adequate amount of brown rice is 2–3% of the food mixture.

Sorghum

Sorghum is a small grain that comes in various sizes and colors, from white to reddish brown. White sorghum is the largest and is probably the most nutritious. It is easily digested and has a high starch content. The protein content is low. It is not especially valuable as a pigeon food, but 2–3% can be added to give the diet more variety.

Legumes

Legumes, or pulses, are an important part of a pigeon's diet. They have a greater percentage of protein than the grains and many seeds, and have a lower fiber content. Legumes are essential during the breeding season. The protein in legumes has different amino acids from that of the grains and is necessary to provide a full range of amino acids. Moreover, the mineral content is much higher than that of most cereals.

It is generally believed that the croppers originated from the Old Dutch croppers and the English pouter. The latter breed was first brought to Holland from India by Dutch sailors.
Above left: French cropper; above right: Norwich cropper; below left: English pouter (cropper); below right: Silesian cropper, a middle-sized pouter, characterized by its short legs. This breed was originally developed in Czechoslovakia.

Pigeon Peas

Pigeon peas are the best known legumes used in the pigeon's food mixture. At one time, pigeon enthusiasts fed their birds pigeon peas only, although many birds had an open loft from which they were able to supplement this monotonous diet with seeds and grains from fields and gardens. Pigeon peas are not now considered such a good food for pigeons, especially in the quantities once given. Pigeon peas contain a high proportion of digestible protein (20%). The calcium and phosphorus content is fairly high at 0.14% and 0.45% respectively. Depending on the season, 5–10% of pigeon peas can be included in the diet.

Green Peas

Green peas are the most suitable protein-rich legumes for our pigeons. The protein content, at 19.4%, is somewhat lower than that of pigeon peas, but green peas are very nutritious and more easily digested. In addition, the various vitamins are better represented than in other legumes. Green peas have a good vitamin B content, and contain vitamin E and carotene (provitamin A). Green peas, which are eagerly consumed, should form 50% of the leguminous part of the diet.

Vetch

Vetch seeds contain 21.6% of digestible proteins — higher than in any other component of pigeon feed. Vetch seeds have good mineral content and stimulate the sex drive. Should they get damp, they will turn black and become poisonous, causing serious diarrhea. For variety, a maximum of 5% should be included in the feed mixture; always beware of poor quality!

Maple Peas

In recent years maple peas have become more popular. They come in various sizes and colors (from nearly white to dark gray-brown). In England maple peas are extensively fed, especially to tumblers and form (or structure) varieties. Maple peas are a good average legume with a protein content of about 19% and a fair mineral content, but poor in vitamins. Up to 10% in the food mixture is adequate.

Seeds

Linseed

Linseed has about the same protein content as green peas (19.5%), but a much higher fat content (about 35%). Linseed may be given only in very small quantities. It seems that the fatty acids and their vitamin content have a positive effect on the growth of young birds. Moreover, linseed gives the pigeon smooth and silky plumage.

Canary Grass Seed (White Seed)

The quality of canary grass seed (or white seed) is similar to that of cereals, but the fat content is higher. The mineral content of the husk plays an important part in the development of young pigeons. Again, only small quantities — ½ ounce (14 grams) per day — should be given.

Hemp

Hemp is eagerly consumed by pigeons. It is high in fat and protein and stimulates the sex drive. Feed it only in very small quantities. It is an excellent tidbit treat for pigeons requiring training in preparation for exhibition .

Safflower Seed

Safflower seed is high in protein but also has a very high fat content. Therefore, 1–2% in the food mixture is adequate (more during molt).

Weed Seeds and Chaff

Weed seeds, of good quality, are an excellent tonic for pigeons. About one thimbleful per bird per day can be mixed with a minute quantity of linseed, canary grass seed, and hemp. This will give the birds a supplement of vitamins and minerals that are scarce in the larger grains and legumes.

Why such small quantities? As noted, many of these seeds have a high fat content, too much of which will make aviary pigeons obese. This is, of course, unhealthy. Some varieties of weed seeds also have high fat content. If you can allow your pigeons to fly free, these seeds can be scattered on the ground. With the seeds the birds will take up particles of earth that will provide further trace elements. If it is not possible to allow free flight, provide the birds with upturned grass sod about once a week. You will see how eagerly the birds peck at the grass seeds. Be sure to purchase your tonic seed from a reliable dealer, as such seeds can easily contain a few poisonous varieties. However, the odd poisonous seed does not seem to harm pigeons. Perhaps our domestic pigeons still possess enough instinct to leave toxic seeds alone.

If you have a pigeon loft in the yard and you allow your birds free flight, be aware that they can damage plants and flowers. There are pigeons that love tulips and will eat them down to the stalks. Especially relished are African marigolds, which will be eaten to the ground. If the birds cannot be allowed free flight, you must supply them with greens (celery, spinach, lettuce, chicory, turnip greens, etc.). Sprayed vegetables should be thoroughly washed to remove insecticides. All vegetables are good in principle, but some are low in vitamins and minerals. Curly kale is probably the best green food for pigeons; it is not eaten too eagerly, but will be taken if finely shredded. Brussels sprouts, cauliflower, broccoli, and all kinds of cabbage are bad for pigeons and should be avoided.

Vitamin Supplements

We have already noted that vitamins are essential for the adequate growth and well-being of our pigeons. Tiny amounts of vitamins occur in the different cereals, legumes, seeds, and supplementary foods. Healthy pigeons will be able to utilize the vitamins contained in the food to the greatest advantage; birds in impaired health, however, are less able to utilize the natural vitamins in the food and are likely to develop a deficiency. Such deficiencies can show in various ways, including weak muscles, swollen eyelids, of thin-shelled eggs, etc.

These conditions may be prevented by giving your pigeons a regular amount of synthetic vitamin/mineral supplements. Several kinds of such supplements are available from pet stores and specialist suppliers; but there are a few cautions to note. First, it may be difficult or impossible to distinguish the pigeons that require extra supplements from the healthy ones; secondly, by giving synthetic vitamins, we discourage the pigeons from producing their own from their normal foods. In such cases, the synthetic vitamins are used in the body and the natural ones are passed out with the body wastes. There are occasions when synthetic vitamin preparations are useful for all the pigeons; for example in the winter, when they are receiving too little sunlight (ultraviolet rays from sunlight are absorbed through the pigeon's skin and help it to produce vitamin D, essential for healthy bones). A small amount of cod-liver oil (enough to barely show on the food seeds) can be added to the food, not more than twice a week. Be sure that the cod-liver oil is fresh; if rancid, it will destroy the vitamin E.

Vitamins are divided into two groups: oil-soluble vitamins A, D, E, and K; and water-soluble vitamins B1, B2, B6, B12, and C. The oil-soluble vitamins are dissolved by body fat and can be stored in the liver as a reserve. The water-soluble vitamins are dissolved by body moisture and cannot be stored; therefore they must be available each day, except for vitamin C (see page 32).

Vitamin A

This vitamin encourages growth in young animals and helps provide immunity from diseases. A deficiency of vitamin A produces degeneration of the mucous membranes, which harden, and give pathogenic organisms the chance to invade the body. The fertility of pigeons will diminish and eggs will not develop properly. Vitamin A is contained in green peas, yellow maize, carrots, green vegetables, and cod-liver oil. You can enhance the pigeons' vitamin A supply by giving your birds finely chopped carrot or curly kale.

Vitamin B1

For pigeons vitamin B1 is essential to convert carbohydrates into glycogen for storage in the liver. Vitamin B1 promotes a good appetite, a healthy nervous and digestive system, and helps build up the skeleton. B1 is contained in wheat, green peas, and brown rice. With adequate feeding of the aforementioned seeds, a deficiency is unlikely.

Vitamin B2

This vitamin is essential for the metabolism of proteins, carbohydrates, and fats, and for the adequate functioning of the nervous system and the development of the embryo. It occurs in the same foods as vitamin B1, and is contained in adequate amounts in most cereals and legumes.

Vitamins B6 and B10

Vitamin B6 (pyridoxine) regulates metabolism in the nerves and liver, and is also important for growth. It occurs in all kinds of grains, yeast, and bran. Vitamin B10 (folic acid) prevents anemia and is also found in grains and yeast, as well as in green feed. Birds that are deficient have leg cramps, weaken quickly, and sit on the ground, exhausted.

Vitamin B12

Vitamin B12 is very important. It is the only vitamin containing a metal: cobalt. It is essential for the formation of red blood cells and for growth in the first few weeks of a pigeon's life. It is also necessary for good development of the eggs.

Suitable Food and Proper Feeding

Vitamin B12 is of animal origin and is not found in normal pigeon food. It is, however, contained in chick-rearing food and in black earth.

Vitamin C

Pigeons produce their own vitamin C in the body; in other words, vitamin C is not required in food. It is produced in the liver and helps produce antibodies to fight pathogenic organisms. It works in close relationship with vitamin A; should there be a deficiency of A, the production of C will be diminished.

Vitamin D

Vitamin D could be called the antirickets vitamin. It helps take calcium and phosphorus from the intestines and into the bloodstream, from where they can be used for building the skeleton. Moreover, a deficiency of vitamin D will promote a deficiency of these two minerals. Vitamin D promotes a balance in the calcium/phosphorus ratio. In its most natural form, vitamin D is produced in the body from ultraviolet rays of sunlight. Pigeons kept in a sunny situation during the summer will not develop a deficiency of vitamin D. In the winter, when the ultraviolet rays are much weaker, the pigeons could develop a deficiency of the vitamin. In the winter a pigeon does not require quite so much vitamin D, but must have some to maintain health. We can supplement the diet with a coating of cod-liver oil on seeds. Another source is vitamin preparations. Be sure that this contains vitamin D3 and not D2, which cannot be used by pigeons. Recently an agricultural research establishment discovered that a detectable amount of vitamin D was contained in some cereals. Barley in particular should contain a reasonable amount. This is because the barley develops in direct sunlight and the husk is inadequate to protect the grain from ultraviolet rays. Unless you are certain that your pigeons are receiving an adequate supply of vitamin D in some form, it is a good idea to make barley a substantial part of winter feeding.

Vitamin E

This vitamin is sometimes called the fertility vitamin. A deficiency of vitamin E will render both sexes infertile. The germ of cereal grains and also legumes are rich in vitamin E, especially wheat and maize (corn). Green peas contain almost three times as much vitamin E per pound as wheat and corn. By feeding these foods to your pigeons a deficiency of vitamin E will be out of the question.

Vitamin K

This vitamin is necessary for the regulation of blood clotting. A deficiency will slow coagulation. However, adequate greens in the diet will prevent any deficiency.

It is worth repeating that you should give your pigeons the most natural and varied menu available, thus avoiding the possibility of a deficiency of "undiscovered vitamins." A diet of varied cereals, seeds, legumes, greens, and minerals will ensure that the pigeon's internal "factory" will have all the necessary materials to produce and maintain a creature in the finest condition.

Pellets and Chick-Rearing Meal

As already mentioned, the vegetable proteins in pigeon food do not supply the quota of amino acids necessary for normal metabolism. Pigeons also need animal proteins to complete the requirements of amino acids. If your pigeons are free-flying, they will be able to find the needed animal supplement, but if they are always kept caged, you will need to supply supplement to the diet.

A few years ago an artificial "grain" was invented. This so-called "expanded-wheat pellet" is manufactured from vegetable and animal proteins, vitamins, minerals, and trace elements, and is very easily digested. The vitamins contained are A, D3, and E, and the raw protein content is approximately 24%. This food has proved excellent.

Suitable Food and Proper Feeding

There are other foods that contain a reasonable percentage of animal protein. Chick-rearing meal is very useful in the breeding season and is eagerly devoured; it is especially beneficial when the young are being reared. A full dish can be given daily; the pigeons will not eat more than is necessary.

Feeding Strategies

Feeding strategies should be changed slightly in the different seasons, such as the resting, breeding, and molting times. In the winter rest period, a small percentage (6–7%) of protein is adequate. The protein is then required only to replace dead body cells and 6–7%, in a varied diet, is enough. Carbohydrates and fats are more important in the rest period, to provide warmth during the colder days and nights.

Preparatory to the breeding season, a couple of weeks before courtship starts, the protein content of the diet must increase, to bring your pigeons into good breeding condition. A few years ago, it was thought that a minimum of 20% protein was necessary at this time, but it is now generally accepted that 12–13% in a varied diet is adequate. If you want 20% protein in the diet, 80% of the food will consist of legumes, producing a protein diet that is too one-sided. Too high a percentage of protein can cause gout and other disabilities.

Newly weaned birds can be given the same diet as the adults. In recently independent young pigeons the flight feathers and muscles are not yet fully developed. The whole body is still maturing. As it is learning to fly, the young pigeon will eat little and often. It is obvious therefore that it should have a full container of varied food at all times.

An average-sized pigeon weighs about 3½ ounces (400 gm). On a daily basis, a pigeon requires $\frac{1}{10}$ to $\frac{1}{12}$ of its body weight in food; that is $\frac{1}{3}$ ounce (30–40 gm) per day. During the rearing of the young the amount can double and during the rest period (if it is not too cold), it may reduce to ¼ ounce (25–30 gm). The $\frac{1}{3}$ ounce (30–40 gm) of food is best given in two parts, mornings and evenings. The best way is to use a hopper as described on page 21.

You can scatter half of the food on the floor. The pigeons will first eat the seeds they like best. To find their favorite seeds in the trough, they will dig with the beak and throw the other seeds all over the place. To prevent this, you can first put the barley in the trough, then the cereals, and finally the legumes on top. After all the pigeons have had their fill, there will usually be some barley left in the bottom of the cup. If there is more than the barley left, you are giving the birds too large a ration, which is not good; you do not want your pigeons too fat. The small amount of barley can be left in the trough, but should be gone by the next feeding time.

Note: *Never* allow croppers to take too much food and water at a time. Excessive eating and drinking can cause "hanging crop" and digestive disorders.

Feeding in the Rest Period

During the winter rest period, no eggs are being laid, no young are being reared, and molting will be over. Food required will be just for the maintenance of the pigeon's body. However, on colder days and nights, the energy requirement will be somewhat greater.

A protein content of 7–8% is adequate. Various cereals contain this amount, but, as cereal proteins are not adequate in themselves, legumes are added to give the necessary variety of amino acids. The following mixture is recommended for the rest period:

50% barley	5% wheat
15% maize (corn)	5% brown rice
5% green peas	5% expanded-wheat pellets
5% maple peas	3% white sorghum
5% rolled oats	2% sunflower seeds

To this, add a small amount of weed (tonic) seeds mixed with linseed, canary grass seed (or white seed), and a very small amount of hemp. In

Suitable Food and Proper Feeding

very cold weather, you can raise the amount of maize (corn) to 25%, reducing the barley by 10%.

Feeding Before and During the Breeding Season

Two weeks before the breeding period starts, we must bring the birds into breeding condition. The diet must again contain more protein to increase the birds' sex drive. Before this, however, the sexes are separated. The barley ration is gradually reduced and the legume ration increased, so that the 7–8% protein content of the rest period reaches 12–13%, with a great variety of foodstuffs. The mixture should be given throughout the growth and rearing of the young.

The following shows a suitable mixture for the breeding season:

20% green peas	10% wheat
10% pigeon peas	7% maple peas
10% maize (corn)	5% brown rice
10% barley	3% vetch
10% rolled oats	3% white sorghum
10% expanded-wheat pellets	2% sunflower seeds

Green peas predominate for their high vitamin content. In addition, give a few tidbit seeds (as in the diet for the rest period), as well as greens such as lettuce, endive, curly kale, and spinach.

After the eggs have been laid, the protein percentage in the diet can be slightly lowered. Many protein foods are heavy and the digestive system, especially the liver, has to work hard. During the first ten days of brooding, the legume content of the diet can be reduced to 20% (15% green peas and 5% maple peas) and the barley increased to 30%. After the ten days, increase the legumes again to 40% and reduce the barley to 10% of the mixture. If you find this too complicated, you can increase the barley 25–30%. During the rearing of the young, feed liberally twice a day, so that food is always available for the adults after feeding the young. Weaned

youngsters require the same mixture as that on which they are reared.

Molting Period

After the year's longest day, in June, the breeding season should stop. The new youngsters can still be fed the breeding mixture, but the adult birds are approaching their main molting period. Pigeons molt the whole year round; in the rest period they shed some down feathers, but in March/April the first flight feathers are molted. The molt continues slowly until the main molting period, which usually starts mid-July to the beginning of August. We can speed up the molt by feeding only barley for a few days. The birds that are still prepared to breed will then lose their drive and go into molt. During the molting period a lower percentage of protein than in the breeding period should be given. A protein content of 10–11% in the diet will be adequate, but through as varied a diet mixture as possible, in order to supply a full quota of amino acids.

A feed mixture suitable for the molting season is as follows:

25% barley	5% pigeon peas
15% green peas	5% brown rice
10% wheat	5% rolled oats
10% maize (corn)	3% vetch
10% expanded-wheat pellets	3% white sorghum
7% maple peas	2% sunflower seeds

Oil-containing seeds such as sunflower, hemp, linseed, cabbage seed, and rape, fed in small quantities during the molting period, will give an improved bloom to the new plumage. Black pigeons with the so-called "beetle-gloss" will particularly benefit from such tonics.

Don't forget the usual tonics and greens! As soon as the last flight feather has dropped, we shift to the diet for the rest period.

In all of these periods, you must not forget to supply the pigeons with a good, varied grit mixture, greens, and, for birds that are not free-flying, fresh, overturned grass sod every week. Do not leave out barley. And do not feed too much!

Remember, too, that pigeons drink immediately after eating, to help them digest their food. Every time you feed your pigeons, inspect the water fountain and be sure it is filled with fresh water, warmed in frosty weather.

When young are being reared, water is essential for both young and adults. If the parent birds were unable to supply the young with adequately softened food, the chicks would soon die. Pigeons,

Pigeons bathing.

unlike most other birds, suck up water and hold their beaks in it the whole time they are drinking.

Note: Like most birds, pigeons love to bathe, especially in the molting period. Young pigeons like to bathe throughout the year.

Bath water also helps maintain humidity during brooding; otherwise the embryos can die in the shell or the shells may become too hard for the young to break out.

Digestion

A hard seed taken in through the beak passes into the buccal cavity, which consists of a hard and a soft part, where saliva is added; in this saliva are materials that begin the digestive process by releasing and breaking down the carbohydrates. Next, the grain goes via the esophagus into the crop, where it is softened in water that the bird has drunk. The crop is really little more than a widening of the esophagus, where the food can be stored for a while and fed in small quantities into the *proventriculus*. In the walls of the *proventriculus*, or glandular stomach, there are glands that release digestive substances. Two important digestive substances are the enzyme pepsin and hydrochloric acid, which together partly digest the proteins. The hydrochloric acid has two more functions; the first is to provide an antiseptic defense against the fungal and bacterial organisms taken up with the food; the second function is to dissolve the calcium salts in the diet. After passing through the *proventriculus* the grain still retains its original form, perhaps swollen from the effect of soaking and the actions of the digestive juices. The grain is not yet ready to be used by the body. The grain is ground up in the *ventriculus* gizzard (muscular stomach), by the action of grit (tiny sharp gravel) in conjunction with the tough ribbed lining of the gizzard. This action turns the grain into a thin porridge that is then fed into the small intestine. This consists of three parts, the duodenum, the jejunum, and the ileum. The duodenum is loop-shaped, with the pancreas contained within the loop. The pancreas passes its enzymes into the esophagus. These enzymes further break down the proteins, carbohydrates, and fats.

Proteins are broken up into amino acids, and carbohydrates into various sugars. The secretion (gall) of the liver, released in the jejunum, splits the fats up into fatty acids and glycerol.

The small intestine's many folds, richly supplied with blood vessels, provide a greatly amplified surface through which the now totally fluid nutrients can be absorbed into the bloodstream. The indigestible remains of the food are passed into the large intestine and excreted via the cloaca—a cuplike shallow chamber, just inside the vent, into which the intestinal, genital, and urinary canals open.

Breeding Pigeons

When the cote or the aviary is ready, we can take steps to obtain our chosen pigeon variety. A good first tip: do not hurriedly buy birds here and there; first patiently find out how you can best obtain good birds (see page 12). If there is a club for a particular pigeon variety, contact the secretary and ask if any member has surplus birds for sale. There are special clubs for many varieties of pigeons. These clubs aim to promote the particular variety, to keep up its standard and, if possible, to improve it by further selective breeding. Each year the clubs usually hold several "breeders' days" when the breeders get together to discuss current breeding problems, how these may be surmounted, and possibilities of improving the breed. If you visit one of these breeders' meetings, particularly in the latter part of the year, the breeders have the most surplus birds available, and there is a fine chance that you will have a choice of good young birds. These breeders' days are informative both for the beginner and the experienced bird fancier. The club issues a so-called "standard" that precisely describes the characteristics of an ideal pigeon of that particular breed. By following the guidelines the breeders attempt to breed birds as close as possible to the ideal standard. Such information is essential to every serious breeder.

It is best not to start with too many breeding pairs: one or two pairs purchased from a good breeder is adequate for the beginner. One color or a couple of related colors such as red and yellow or blue and blue-silver is best. Try to breed the offspring of these pairs. At the end of the breeding season you will then have a reasonable selection. A good rule to remember is: "The value of a pigeon is judged by the quality of its offspring." The breeding value of a pair can really be determined only after a fair number of offspring have been produced.

The newly purchased birds have the time from autumn to the breeding season to become accustomed to their new accommodation. Study the birds carefully and determine their good and bad points in relation to the standard. Initially you may have time to visit shows that are usually organized in the winter months. At such shows you can learn a lot from the experiences of others.

After a time, you may also want your birds to compete with those of other breeders of that particular breed. Get into conversations with these breeders; they will usually be pleased to give you useful tips on breeding, exhibiting, and other relevant matters.

Young birds hatched in the spring must be ringed with official closed leg bands. These bands are issued by the specialist clubs of the particular breeds. Local clubs are often mixed clubs, including breeders of other animals, such as rabbits and bantam fowl. In some cities there may be clubs that have only pigeon breeders as members. If you are less interested in other kinds of animals, the pigeon club is what you want. Such clubs usually convene monthly meetings with guest speakers on such subjects as feeding, breeding, genetics, and various pigeon breeds. In addition, an annual exhibition is organized, as well as a "young bird exhibition" in the fall. Once a member of such a club, you can request a breeder's card and bands.

The Breeding Season

The sexes are separated from mid-February to the beginning of March, or in suitable weather conditions, even earlier, and you can slowly increase the protein content of the diet (see page 33). The breeding boxes must be prepared. You can allow the pigeons to build their own nests by providing them with straw or tobacco stalks. Tobacco stalks are perhaps better, as straw is slippery and may have sharp ends that could damage the eggs. Easily cleaned porcelain nest pans can be provided in which the birds will build their nests. The porcelain pans have the disadvantage of being too cold in the early part of the year; they remove too much heat from the nest. This can be overcome with a thick layer of newspaper in the nest pan, then some tobacco stalks over the paper. This will act as a good insulator; as a bonus, the newspaper ink may help deter lice. If the nest becomes too bulky, simply remove the newspaper and some of the tobacco stalks. Another kind of nest pan can be made of wood. A square box 10 × 10 inches (25 × 25 cm) with 2-inch (5-cm) sides can be used (see page 22). For large breeds it should measure 12 × 12 inches (30 × 30 cm).

As the newly introduced pair must spend many days in the breeding compartment, food and water

A nest pan. Pet dealers also sell paper nest bowls which are disposable after use.

containers must be included as described in the chapter on housing (see page 21). Double food containers consisting of two porcelain pots joined together are available. These are very practical and ideal for the breeding compartment. Do not forget to provide a separate dish with grit.

Record cards can be affixed to the breeding compartments and such data as the ring numbers of the parents, the date of egg laying, the date of hatching, and the ring numbers of the offspring can be recorded. This will ensure that at the end of the breeding season you know the parentage of each chick.

The cocks can be let loose in the breeding facility or confined in the breeding compartments. If free, the cocks will usually fight for what they consider the best compartments (usually the highest

and darkest ones); the outcome is usually that the strongest cock will get the best compartment, leaving the others in peace for the rest of the season. If the cocks are confined to the compartments, there is the chance that the strongest cock is confined to a lower compartment. When let out, he will still try for the higher compartments, and this will lead to much fighting!

After two or three weeks the hens are introduced to the cocks in the breeding compartments. Pairing usually takes place immediately, but there are some breeds that are a little more "difficult." Should pairing not be successful, for instance when the cock drives the hen away, the pair can be placed in the so-called "pairing cage." This is a double cage with a mesh division. After a few days the cock will show a desire to get to the hen. If introduced to each other and all goes well, they are as good as paired and can be returned to the breeding compartment. The breeding pairs should be kept together in the breeding compartments for a few days to become accustomed to each other and to the nest box. Open the breeding compartments in turn, so that the pair knows how to find its way back to its own nest. There must be good discipline in the breeding facility; we do not want cocks going into other compartments later and disturbing the broods.

Eggs

After pairing and as long as the weather is not too cold, we can expect the first eggs within ten days. The first egg is usually laid in the evening between 5PM and 7PM. Young hens often lay smaller than average eggs and these may have a little blood on the shell. This is no big concern; if they have been fertilized, they will develop normally. The second egg is laid about 43 to 44 hours later, usually in the afternoon between 2PM and 3PM. After the second egg is laid, serious brooding commences. Sometimes brooding starts after the first egg, and if you do not notice this in time, the first egg will hatch about 36 hours before the second one. The first chick will then be nearly twice the size of the newly-hatched second chick. The larger and stronger first chick will get most of the food, and the second chick will be neglected. If no steps are taken to rectify the matter, the neglected chick will either die or grow up as a runt. To prevent this problem remove the first egg from the nest and replace it when the second egg has been laid. Keep the first egg in a cool, dark place on a layer of soft paper tissue.

Brooding

The hen broods from approximately 4PM to 10 AM. The cock broods the rest of the time. After five days the eggs should be inspected to see if they are fertile. The eggs are carefully removed from the nest and "candled" by holding the egg against a hole in a piece of cardboard in front of a bright light in a dark room. If fertile, you will be able to see the embryo and blood vessels through the thin shell. Infertile, the eggs will be "clear." Depending on the weather, the incubation time is 14–18 days.

During the brooding time both the cock and the

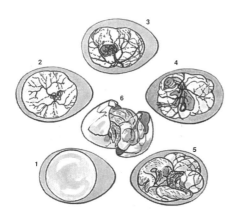

Stages of embryo development.

1. Fresh-laid egg	4. 10th day
2. 3rd day	5. 15th day
3. 7th day	6. Hatching chick

hen develop the so-called "pigeon milk" in the crop. This starts on about the tenth to twelfth day. The marvelous thing is that it occurs in both sexes, as a result of the action of the pituitary hormone prolactin, similar to the hormone that promotes milk in mammals. Pigeon's milk is a soft, cheeselike secretion produced on the walls of the crop. It has a protein content of 14–16% and a fat content of 8–10%; it contains minerals and vitamins, but no carbohydrates. On the 17th and 18th days the "milk" production is at its high point and stays like that for 7 or 8 days; then it begins to reduce until no more is produced after about 12 days. From the sixth day, the "milk" is mixed with seed to give to the young. This is necessary to wean the chicks to solid food.

Hatching

The chicks hatch in 17 or 18 days. On top of the beak is the so-called "egg tooth," a hornlike projection that the chick uses to break open the shell. By twisting and turning in the shell and the use of the egg tooth the chick breaks out of the shell. In a few days, the egg tooth will be absorbed and no longer be visible. From the first pecking open of the shell to complete hatching can take 15–30 hours. Within a few hours of the hatchlings drying out, they receive their first meal of "milk" from the parents.

Some eggs may be chipped, but the chicks may not hatch. Sometimes a hole is pecked in the shell and you can see the chick and hear it peeping, but it does not make further progress in hatching. It is possible that the chick is too weak to turn in the shell and break it open, or that the shell contents dry out too quickly. If too dry, the chick will adhere to the inside of the shell and be unable to move. If we do not take steps to rectify the situation, the chick will die.

There are two things we can do. First, the of the shell can be gently removed so that the chick's head is free—but do absolutely nothing more. Replace

Breeding Pigeons

the egg in the nest, but keep an eye on it! A second possibility is to put a little of your saliva into the hole in the egg — the saliva is warm and slippery — and return the egg to the nest. If the chick is healthy, it should be able to hatch safely. This does not sound very nice, but it works!

During hatching, the birds should be disturbed as little as possible. If the parents are not too shy or too aggressive, we can allow ourselves a careful little look; otherwise wait to look in the nest when the parent birds leave the eggs to feed.

When the chick hatches, it takes a few hours to dry; then the parents very carefully give the first food in small amounts at a time. The young pigeon grows amazingly quickly, and doubles its birth weight in 48 hours. In 32 to 35 days it will be fully developed, able to fly and feed itself. In this time, most of the plumage forms and a strong skeleton develops so that the bird is soon able to care for itself.

The Young

After two weeks the young are left alone in the nest for longer periods, especially during the day. At this time, the plumage will be developing well and we will be able to see the colors of the young pigeon. The hen will ignore the chicks more frequently and the parental pair will be preparing for the next brood. This can be a critical period for the chicks; they can be neglected when the cock forces the hen to sit on the new nest until the next egg is laid. The best solution to this is to shut the pair up in the breeding compartment with the chicks and the second nest pan. This is placed higher than the first pan, so that when the chicks start moving about, they do not damage the new eggs.

After 14 to 18 days the cock mainly cares for the chicks alone. As discussed in the chapter on feeding, the birds must receive a larger ration of food at this time. Food and water dishes can be placed in the breeding compartment. The advantage of this is that the youngsters will see the adults eating and drinking, and will be encouraged to peck up some food or drink some water themselves. After about 30 days the youngsters will begin to take a greater interest in the world outside the breeding compartment; they will start to spread their wings and practice flying. Sometimes, a youngster will accidentally fall to the ground while doing this. You must watch out for this, as other cock birds may attack the fallen chick or even attempt to copulate with it, or kill it.

A few smaller shelves can be placed against the lower walls of the cote, so that any youngster that has fallen out of the breeding compartment can hide until you rescue it. It can be dangerous for a youngster if it tries to fly back to its compartment. If it should land in the wrong one, it will be fiercely pecked by the inmates and could be severely injured or even killed if it cannot escape quickly enough. It is therefore important that the young become independent as early as possible. From the 25th to 30th day of age the young can be placed for a few hours each day in a juvenile compartment. They are not likely to eat in strange surroundings. The youngsters can be left in this compartment for one to two hours longer each day, but they should be returned to their home in the evening, so that they can be fed by the cock, and go to sleep with a full crop. As soon as they are independent and can feed themselves they can be removed permanently to the juvenile compartment; by this time they will already have become accustomed to it and they will already know where the food and water containers are. This process is necessary to ensure that the young pigeons get a good start without suffering too much stress in the new surroundings. Shy varieties in particular may have some difficulties in settling into new accommodations.

The "nest plumage" is somewhat different from the adult plumage, but the experienced breeder can tell if the right colors have been bred. With some patterned breeds, even as the first feathers appear, one can see if the plumage is growing correctly and whether there is too much or too little white in the plumage. Some color breeds can go through a complete color metamorphorsis at the first molt.

After seven to eight weeks, the first primary feathers will appear and the bird will soon take on its adult colors and markings. At this time the young birds require peace and rest. In addition, they need sunlight and a balanced diet. On sunny days, they will spread their wings in order to catch as much of the sun's rays as possible.

The birds will also like to bathe. A plastic or enamel dish of suitable diameter and 4–6 inches (10–15 cm) high is ideal. Young pigeons are crazy about bathing and even very young ones will be encouraged to bathe when they see the older pigeons doing so. Bath water must be clean and should be changed after each use. It has been said that this bathing is not necessarily good for their health, but when you see how much pleasure the birds get from dunking themselves in clean water and allowing as much water as possible to run through their feathers, you can hardly believe this is not also healthful. It probably stimulates feather growth.

After bathing, the plumage is groomed with the beak, promoting good blood circulation. Bathing is also a health indicator; sick birds do not bathe!

Young pigeons are very gregarious. There can be a few minor squabbles but these are brief, and love soon prevails again. It is wrong to raise young pigeons in solitude. By nature pigeons are colony birds that like each other's company. When they are sexually mature it may seem that they have changed their behavior. Cock birds can get into some violent fights, but as soon as each knows his place, things will settle again. Pigeons in a particular cote know each other well, but if a new bird is introduced, all of the inmates will look at it as if to ask: "What do you want here?" This can also be seen in the juvenile pen when new pigeons are introduced.

Just like dogs, pigeons have a hierarchal system. The dominant cocks in a cote or aviary have the best perches, and no other pigeon is allowed to use them. Pigeons become very attached to their own perches. A bird on a high perch will fiercely defend it from any bird that attempts to take possession of it. The same applies to the nest boxes and breeding compartments; they are aggressively defended against intruders.

Fostering and Leg Banding

Some breeders like to remove one of the chicks to another pair of pigeons as foster parents, believing that a pair can feed a single chick better. However, a healthy pair of pigeons should easily be able to rear two chicks. They are perfectly equipped to do this. Moreover, two chicks in a nest can keep each other warm, especially in the spring, when the days can still be cold. At ten days old, when the young are nicely quilled, the parents will leave the nest at dawn and the two chicks will keep each other warm.

Some breeders have another method, in which they lengthen the time that crop milk is given. They remove the youngsters at about six days of age to another nest, where the eggs are at point of hatching. The eggs are removed. The young pigeons then receive an extra seven days of crop milk from the foster parents. The young are then supposed to be much stronger. This method is, however, also not necessary. The pigeon's body is equipped to work best from the normal feeding cycle as supplied by its parents and should develop healthily in the most natural manner.

Depending on the breed, the chicks must be leg-banded between the fifth and tenth day. Feather-footed breeds are ringed after five days; smooth-legged varieties after about seven days, and all other breeds with leg and foot feathers after ten days. The ring (band) should rest on the heel and not on the upper leg. The ring should be inspected for the first few days to ensure that it is sitting properly and not interfering with growth.

Sometimes it may be necessary to transfer chicks to another pair for fostering. This can be done up to the age of about 14 days, but should not be done once the youngsters are fully feathered, as they will not be accepted. Some pairs may more

Breeding Pigeons

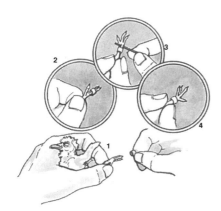

Banding a week-old squab (chick).
1. Preparing to slip the ring on (while holding back one toe).
2. Three toes enclosed by the band.
3. After pushing the band down, pull out the fourth toe with a toothpick.

readily accept older chicks than others. If a chick is not accepted by any foster parents, it will be necessary to hand-rear it (see also pages 33 and 34). The food is soaked in water for a few hours to soften the grains, seeds, and legumes. The softened food is then rinsed in warm water to bring it to body temperature; this then approximates food given by pigeon parents. The softened food is offered into the chick's beak with a plastic spoon at least three times per day. After a few attempts, you can become quite an expert. No extra water should be given, unless the bird shows thirst by flickering the eyes; then a small amount can be dropped into the beak. Too much water can interfere with the food/water balance. The best way is to let the chick drink by itself, by holding its beak in a dish of water.

Selection and Pairing

The two most important elements of our hobby are selection and correct pairing. The experienced breeder who can select good pairs and produce top youngsters year after year has a great advantage over other fanciers. All other factors, such as cote furnishings, feeding, rearing, etc. are purely technical and can soon be learned. Of course, selection can and must also be learned; there are a few basic rules, but there is more to it than that. As a good gardener must have a "green thumb" a top pigeon breeder must have something similar—a "sixth sense." If at all possible, take the opportunity to visit and see how a top breeder operates. You may see birds that will astonish you and make you ask: "Why is that one being kept?" The breeder may be using a bird that has failed in exhibition because of a particular fault, but that has some very good qualities useful to the breed. The imperfect bird may be a mother or grandmother of a bird that is the handsomest of the current breeding season!

The first priority in selection is health and vitality. The selection starts during hatching. A chick must hatch in the normal manner without the artificial help described earlier (see page 38). Leaving aside exceptions (such as breeds with very short beaks) you can usually see at hatching if the chick can be a pigeon of prime quality.

A healthy hatchling is fed by the adults after a few hours and lies with its head held up between the breast feathers of the adult. The youngster, or squab, grows extremely quickly in the first week and must have a permanently full crop. We can tell if the parents are feeding crop milk or solid food as the milk colors the chick's crop yellow. We must ensure that the changeover from crop milk to solid food between the seventh and tenth days occurs without difficulty. Some squabs that receive insufficient carbohydrates can develop metabolic problems, indicated by greenish droppings rather than the usual gray-brown color. To be able to compare the growth of youngsters it is advisable to plan as many eggs as possible to be laid and hatched at the same time. We can then see which squabs are growing faster than the others. Healthy young will be fully feathered in 14 days and able to maintain their own body warmth, especially during the day and when there are two chicks in the nest.

The next stage in selection comes as the young pigeons are weaned. At the 7th week, the birds will begin to molt and the adult plumage will begin to form. They will bathe regularly. If all this goes well, vitality is not a serious concern.

Later, when the pigeons choose their permanent perches, the healthiest and strongest specimens will take possession of the highest perches. This also is a clue to the best birds for breeding. To build up a stud it is essential to choose the strongest and healthiest birds for breeding.

After selection for vitality, the next step is selection for breed standard. Here are a few general rules.

With each breed it is important to separate general rules of the standard from minor ones and not to become confused with small details. The general standards should always be kept within the breed. As an example: the standard for the Old Dutch owl asks for a shape and stance, as well as for a good beak and head, excellent color and markings. It is obvious that shape and stance are the most important features, and you must select with this in mind. Birds with a wide breast, short abdomen, and a well-balanced stance are what we are looking for. Second in importance are a strong, well-positioned beak, a good head profile with a long forehead and a flat top. Then come color and markings, which must not be too hard and must be properly distributed over the body.

There are special standards for each breed. Many beginners and even some more experienced breeders buy a pair of prize birds and expect their young to be winners too. In such cases one often has disappointing results; the young have none of the good qualities of the adults, and you wonder why.

What conformation make a pigeon a winner? In most cases it is a bird with the best *overall* conformation. In other words, it has all the necessary requirements of the standard, but without excelling in them. An Old Dutch owl, for example, with a very good shape and stance, a very well-positioned beak and a very good head profile, with good color and markings, will achieve a high award at an exhibi-

tion, possibly the best of the breed. There will be other birds with not all the requirements of the standards as good as those of the winner, but they may have individual points that are better than those of the winner of our example. A bird may have a wide breast, but it can lose points by being longer in the abdomen, or by having a small fault in the markings. Such a bird will obviously receive a lesser award or no award at a show, but it still can be an excellent breeding pigeon. Another bird can have an ideal shape and stance with a short abdomen, but can be stronger in the beak. Two such birds can make an ideal breeding pair. Successful pigeon breeding depends on careful selection of pairs, in which either bird provides what the other may be lacking. The perfect "standard pigeon," however — one that has all the requirements of that standard — does not exist.

Never buy a mediocre bird; select one that shows high quality in one or more breed-standard requirements, and try to find a mate that shows good points that the first bird lacks. This method has a greater chance of success. Never breed a pair that have the same faults, as these may intensify in the offspring. Each pairing must have a definite goal; the desire to breed better birds.

It is also desirable to breed as many birds as possible of a particular breed, so that you can learn by experience. Study all possibilities offered by a particular breed; discuss the breed with other fanciers, breeders, and experts; never be satisfied with a single success, but strive for further improvement. You can never know everything; there are always new things to learn. It is difficult to breed a top bird in the breed, but even more difficult to continue breeding top birds!

Breeding Methods

There are different methods for breeding pigeons. One of these is so-called "linebreeding." Linebreeding consists of pairing youngsters back to parents and sometimes brother to sister. This can also be referred to as "inbreeding," a word that some breeders like to avoid. It is thought that inbreeding can weaken the strain to the extent that after a few generations the pigeons are no longer fertile, or suffer birth defects. The truth is that *careful* inbreeding, coupled with good management, can produce generations of fine birds.

With linebreeding, selection for excellent health and vitality is important. Any bird with the smallest imperfection should not be used for this breeding method. Linebreeding of father to daughter or son to mother has the aim of cutting out as much variation as possible and at the same time producing a line in which each bird is as close as possible to the ideal standard for the breed. It is selective breeding in which over a period of time all undesirable elements in the strain are suppressed. This method of breeding requires expert knowledge, especially in the selection of ideal birds.

In another breeding method two pairs of birds are selected from various breeders. These birds must show good standard requirements. These pairs then are bred at the same time. Only the best youngsters from each mating are used to further the stud; the poor-quality chicks are not bred. Selection depends first on condition and secondly on breed standard requirements. The good young are paired as much as possible to good birds from the other pair. After a time, you have a stud that is not so *closely* related as with linebreeding, but are slightly *more distantly* related.

How to Keep Pigeons Healthy

In general, pigeons are fairly resistant to diseases, but since they are often kept together in relatively small accommodations, the chance of an epidemic is somewhat greater than for birds living in the wild.

Prevention is always better than cure! The conscientious pigeon fancier will ensure that water, grit, and other containers are regularly cleaned of dirt and droppings, that the food is protected from dust and vermin, and that the floors, platforms, perches, and nest boxes — all parts of the pigeon house — are kept scrupulously clean.

As we have already discussed in the chapter on housing, drafts are probably the main enemy of pigeons (and other birds), so doors and windows on opposite sides of the cote should never be open at the same time. A good pigeon fancier will examine each bird daily at feeding time; should there be birds that have lost their appetite, are uneasy and peck at other birds, or sit with fluffed feathers, they should be isolated and observed for disease symptoms. This will help prevent an epidemic in the whole stock.

Should the disease be unrecognizable, do not hesitate to consult a veterinarian who specializes in avian medicine. The average fancier is not a doctor and is unlikely to know about the most recent developments in veterinary medicine. Your pigeon club will be able to recommend a suitable veterinarian.

Egg Binding

Egg binding is usually caused by an infection of the oviduct or the ovary in the female pigeon. Young females are especially susceptible to the condition. Soft shells, double-yolked eggs, or broken eggs in the oviduct can also cause a similar problem. The sick female sits in the nest with fluffed feathers and gives the impression that she is dying. A hard swelling caused by an egg that cannot be laid can be felt in the lower abdomen. If a

A hospital cage.

lukewarm bath does not help, the bird should be wrapped in a woolen cloth (with just the head free). The warmth will promote blood circulation and help the egg to be laid. In severe cases an avian veterinarian should be consulted.

Soft-shelled eggs

The cause of soft-shelled eggs is an infection or a malformation of part of the oviduct. The egg's hard calcareous shell is absent; only the membranelike inner "shell" covers the egg. A deficiency of calcium, grit, and sand over a long period will cause the same problem. Females that continually lay soft-shelled eggs are useless for breeding.

Trichomoniasis

This disease is caused by a single-celled flagellated protozoan parasite — *Trichomonias columbae*. Other names for the disease include "canker," "diphtheria," and "frounce," the last one in particu-

All four varieties on this page are Danish tumblers. The breed originated in Denmark and is characterized by the long and slender neck, body, legs, beak and head. One of the most striking and oldest varieties is the Danish tiger tumbler (above right). All four pictures were taken shortly after these birds received highest honors during a Danish Pigeon Show in 1988.

lar in birds of prey that probably contract the disease by eating infected pigeons. Symptoms of this disease include yellow, buttonlike lesions on the epithelium in the mouth, esophagus, and crop. Besides raptors and pigeons, many other birds are susceptible to the disease, especially chickens and turkeys. Research has shown that at least 80% of all pigeons are infected. Many older birds are carriers of the disease, but are themselves not affected by its symptoms. Young pigeons are the main victims of the disease. Juveniles from one to five weeks of age can acquire the disease from their carrier pigeons via the crop milk and will soon die. The infection can also invade the navel before it has healed from detachment from the yolk stalk. Once infected, the patient becomes lethargic after one week, fluffs its plumage, and has serious digestive problems, including diarrhea. The infected bird will quickly lose weight and drink profusely, sitting with outstretched neck (penguin stance), gasping for breath. The three forms of the disease are:

Mouth Cavity Form: Cheeselike yellow lesions, sometimes as large as a bean, occur on the mucous membranes of the mouth. The bird will have difficulty in breathing and eating. In serious cases, the lesions grow so large as to stick out of the edges of the beak.

Navel Form: Infected crop milk that falls into the nest pan can infect the unhealed navel of a squab. A swelling occurs under the skin around the navel, which, on examination, appears cheeselike and crumbly.

Organ Form: Both of the above forms can infect other internal organs. For example, cheeselike lesions on the liver.

Above left and right: The satinette, an Oriental frill, is closely related to the owls.
Center left: The German shield owl.
Center right: The Chinese owl.
Below left: The African owl.
Below right: The Antwerp smerle.

Treatment: The disease requires 4–14 days from infection to the appearance of symptoms and can be treated with various medications, including aminotrothiazole and dimetridazone; the latter shows excellent results. Of course, prevention is better than cure! It is therefore recommended that before the breeding season, with advice from your veterinarian, all birds be given prophylactic treatment via the drinking water so that any trichomonias present are destroyed.

Coccidiosis

Coccidiosis, an intestinal disease, is also caused by a protozoan parasite, usually *Eimeria labbeana* or *E. columbarum*. The life cycle of the single-celled parasite is quite complicated; it will suffice to say that the protozoans infect the cells in the intestinal walls in large numbers, multiply there and eventually destroy the individual cells. Each time a cell is destroyed, protozoa are released into the intestine, infect the semi-digested food, and attack new cells. One form of the parasite is passed out in the feces and is called an oocyst.

The seriousness of the infection will depend on the numbers of protozoa. Seriously infected pigeons rapidly lose weight, and their droppings are watery. No blood appears in the pigeon's droppings, as is the case with infected chickens.

The oocysts released in the droppings can only develop further if ingested by another pigeon, but only "ripe" oocysts will develop. The ripening takes place best in a damp and warm environment. It should be noted that pigeons can be infected only by ripe oocysts of pigeon coccidia, and not those of other animals. In order to prevent this disease, you must thus keep the cote scrupulously clean and dry and protect it from infected birds. Unfortunately there is not yet a sure cure for this disease.

Treatment: There are preventive medicines that can be mixed in the drinking water. In serious cases, a cure should be given with the assistance of

How to Keep Pigeons Healthy

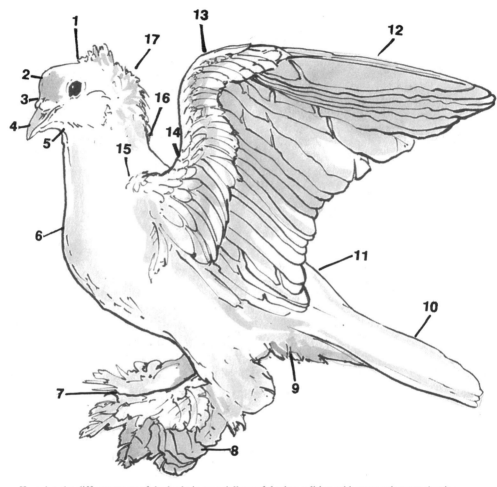

Knowing the different parts of the body is especially useful when talking with your avian veterinarian.

1. crown, or topskull
2. frontal, or forehead
3. nostril cere, or wattle
4. beak (upper and lower mandible)
5. chin, and bib (throat) region
6. crop region
7. foot
8. foot feathers
9. vent region
10. tail
11. rump and upper (dorsal) tail coverts
12. wing
13. wrist, or wing butt
14. elbow
15. shoulder
16. nape
17. back skull with crest

an avian veterinarian. A fecal examination one week after the last treatment is strongly recommended.

If an epidemic occurs, steam cleaning of the entire pigeon facility in combination with proper medication of the entire flock can get things back under control. It is believed by many researchers who work with coccidiosis that this condition is most likely incurable, but that it can be kept under control through good husbandry.

Since stress can produce an outbreak of the condition, it is important to check birds that are stressed at shows to be certain that the condition does not show up following such stress. A fecal examination should be made within three to five days following the show. Show birds should also be isolated from the flock for a period of at least five days following a show. If the oocysts appear in examined feces, the birds may then be treated prior to reintroduction to the main flock, and the coccidiosis brought back under control.

It is an excellent idea to erect an isolation cote, completely separated from the regular cote, for the quarantine of sick birds or birds coming home from shows. Ideally such a cote would be erected at a good distance from the regular cote, and constructed to withstand steam cleaning. There are professional steam cleaners who could come to the facility, or steam cleaners can be rented.

Pox

Pox infections are caused by a virus that attacks the skin and mucous membrane cells. In external pox an infected pigeon will have crusty lesions on its unfeathered parts, especially around the eyes, around the beak, on the feet, and around the anus. The mucous membrane form (the internal form: diphtheria) is recognized by a cheeselike, evil-smelling deposit in the beak and throat cavities. It is possible for one individual pigeon to have both forms of the disease.

The pox virus is transmitted via saliva droplets from the nose and mouth, seldom via the droppings. The infection is picked up with food or water or by a mosquito bite; keep mosquitoes out of the cote. The virus may also be present in dust that, when inhaled, infects the bird. During pigeon transport or at exhibitions, sometimes pigeons tend to squabble, and small injuries result. The pox virus can then easily gain entry into the bloodstream. Infected wild pigeons can also transmit the disease.

The first visible signs that a bird is infected occur after 4–14 days. In one example, the virus can enter the bloodstream through a wound. The virus multiplies quickly and infects the liver and bone marrow, from whence it reinfects the blood. Via the blood, the pox organisms then migrate to the skin and mucous membranes, forming lesions that are a good feeding ground for many bacteria, such as staphylococci and streptococci. Thus pus soon forms. Do not confuse pox with trichomoniasis. Also do not confuse a pox infection with a vitamin A deficiency, which causes a change in the membrane of the eyelid. Especially do not confuse pox with ornithosis, which causes a profuse watering of the eyes and thus causes the surrounding feathers to stick together.

Treatment: As there is no treatment vaccine available to date, the patient should be treated with antibiotics such as chlortetracycline, spectinomycine, or mycosan-t, in order to combat possible secondary bacterial infection. In addition, a vitamin preparation should be administered (especially vitamin A to promote skin healing) and arsanil-acid to increase body resistance.
• In a serious outbreak of pox the deposit on the skin and mucous membranes must be removed daily.
• A 0.5 ml injection of salmosan-t must be given — obviously only by an avian veterinarian — in the skin (in the neck or breast). In serious cases the injection should be given three times, at eight-hour intervals.
• Treat each healthy pigeon with chlortetracycline for 4–7 days. Also give 7.5 gm chlortetracycline per gallon of drinking water.

• Disinfect the cote at least twice, with a week between treatments.

• Continue chlortetracycline treatment for four weeks, with advice from a veterinarian. A pigeon that recovers from a pox infection is immune for life.

• Prevent infection by immunization. Young pigeons can be immunized from the age of six weeks. Three or four feathers are removed from the thigh, and the serum is applied to the hair follicles with a small, stiff-haired brush. Pox viruses are different in various animals and humans. Thus there is chicken pox, pigeon pox, and canary pox, as well as human ("chicken") pox. Pigeons can develop chicken pox (although usually in a milder form), but not canary pox. An infected pigeon is not dangerous to humans.

Ornithosis

Ornithosis is caused by *Chlamydomonas*, a group of organisms with characteristics of both viruses and bacteria. However, since bacteria and mycoplasmata can also be responsible for infections and changes in the mucous membranes of the eyes, nose, throat, and intestines, we generally speak of an "ornithosis-complex," or o-c. The disease is not fatal to fully grown pigeons. Isolated patients will quickly respond if placed in a warm, draft-free cage and will in a few days or weeks be their old selves again. The disease is transmittable from an infected bird to humans; an affected person must consult a doctor immediately. O-c, as it occurs in humans, can be best compared with the flu, although the cause is a totally different virus.

O-c is caused by various chlamydomonas which, in general, occur in many pigeon cotes, and under normal circumstances do not present a great danger. But should the birds suffer from stress (molting, exhibitions, bad food, cold and damp in the loft, drafts, etc.) they become more susceptible to a heavy o-c infection. If a bird should be infected by an additional disease, then the danger is also greater. A bird suffering from o-c is less inclined to fly, a symptom that also occurs in many other diseases. After a time, the bird will develop respiratory problems, will quickly tire, and sit with open beak gasping for breath. Thereafter, the normally white or light rose-colored eyelid membranes will swell and become gray or brown. The eyes water profusely, and an inflamed, wet patch soon forms under the eyes. In serious cases the eyelids will stick together, and secondary bacterial infections can cause blindness. The nostrils become gray and are also wet from a running nose. The bird will sneeze and scratch at its face. Should the mucous membranes of the nose, throat, and trachea become infected, the bird will sit with open beak, gasping for breath. As the trachea fills with mucus, you may hear a rattling sound as the bird gasps. The intestines may become infected, resulting in diarrhea.

O-c is very infectious, it can be transmitted via infected drinking water and also through the air. Do not allow overcrowding in the cote. The cote must be well ventilated, clean and light, and disinfected at least once a week. Damp, stagnant air will spread the disease more quickly.

Never place fully grown pigeons with youngsters, which are much more susceptible to o-c.

Treatment: You can do two things: 1. Allow the birds to be injected by a vet: 0.5 ml oxytetracycline in the breast muscle; repeat after 24 hours and 2. administer suanovil-aureomycin or chlortetracycline in the drinking water. In all cases, consult your avian veterinarian.

O-c should not be confused with mycoplasmosis, where the infection of the eyelids does not occur. Also, a cold in the eye should not be confused with o-c; a cold in the eye soon passes and is recognizable through the infection of the conjunctiva. Such an infection can also be caused by pasteurellosis (a bacterial disease).

As already mentioned, o-c is also transmittable to humans. It resembles a kind of influenza with fever, which can last for one to two weeks. Consult a doctor immediately for treatment with antibiotics.

How to Keep Pigeons Healthy

Mycoplasmosis

Mycoplasmosis is caused by tiny microscopic organisms (mycoplasmata) and does not infect pigeons only, but also turkeys and other poultry. Often occurring at the same time as o-c, mycoplasmosis is transmitted from pigeon to pigeon through droppings in water and food. It is suspected that almost all pigeons are infected with the organism, but it usually bothers only active homing pigeons. One to two weeks after the initial infection, you may note a watery nasal discharge, which later develops into a slimy pus-containing discharge. A grayish deposit appears in the beak and the saliva is tough and hangs wirelike between tongue and palate. There is swelling in the infected beak and throat cavity; an unhealthy smell is apparent. The nostrils become gray. If you press the nostrils, a thick discharge emerges. As the air passages become congested, breathing becomes labored; the patient sits with open beak and makes wheezing noises, especially in the evenings and at night. The air sacs can also be infected.

A strong mucous discharge also occurs with ornithosis, though in mycoplasmosis there is not usually an infection of the eyelid. Fatalities rarely occur, although the disease usually has a long duration. A veterinarian should be consulted.

Treatment: Serious cases require a subcutaneous injection of 0.5 ml salmosan-t in the neck, or intramuscularly in the breast muscles. Repeat after 6–12 hours if necessary. All healthy pigeons of the same loft should be treated with erythromycin, spiromycin, mycosan-t, or similar medicines (of course, under the guidance of a veterinarian!). Thoroughly clean and disinfect the whole cote, preferably on a weekly schedule.

Salmonella or Paratyphus

Salmonella causes many fatalities in young pigeons. The rodlike salmonella enterobacteria (bacteria found mainly in the intestines) cause problems with the bone joints, diarrhea, and nervous problems. They cause paratyphus in mammals (including humans) and various birds. In general, the disease is not fatal, as long as a veterinarian is consulted in time.

The bacteria are passed in the droppings of infected birds, or via the crop-milk, the saliva, or infected eggs. It is well known that certain unaffected pigeons can be carriers, constantly endangering the whole pigeon stock. Birds are infected by ingesting food or water contaminated by the droppings of infected birds. Infected parent birds can infect their young through feeding them. An infection is also possible through breathing infected air. Infected females can infect the eggs through an infected ovary. Salmonella organisms can enter the eggs within two days. There are four forms of the disease, which can all infect at the same time:

Intestinal Form: The bacteria enter the walls of the intestine. Diarrhea is a result, with foul-smelling, soupy, green or brown droppings surrounded by slime and containing undigested food particles. A green color in the droppings can also indicate a gall infection. Consult a veterinarian immediately!

Joint Form: A strong intestinal infection can result in the bacteria entering the bloodstream and infecting all parts of the body, including the bone joints. The result is an overproduction of joint lubricant, causing intense swelling. The patient attempts to relieve the intense pain by not using the wings and the feet.

Organ Form: Once the bacteria enter the bloodstream they can infect all internal organs, especially the liver, kidneys, pancreas, heart, and various other glands. The sick bird becomes inactive, mopes in a corner of the cote, becomes short of breath and nearsighted.

Nervous Form: Salmonella can infect the nerves and spinal column. The infection spreads along the sinews and causes imbalance and crippling. The turning of the neck, fouling of the cloaca, and cramplike contractions of the toes are typical symptoms.

How to Keep Pigeons Healthy

Pigeons infected with salmonella bacteria get serious intestinal problems in four to five days. The bacteria multiply in the intestinal lining and eventually migrate into the bloodstream. Fatalities occur quickly in young birds, because they have no immunity. Older birds, however, incubate the disease over a long period, and if they are not adequately cured, they will become carriers capable of infecting other birds via their oviducts and their droppings.

Heavy losses of young birds during the breeding season are a sign of salmonellosis in the stock. The sick birds will have heavy diarrhea and suffer from leg and wing disablement. A veterinarian should be called immediately to examine blood samples and dead birds.

Do not confuse salmonellosis with thread or roundworm infestation or coccidiosis. Examination of the feces will show whether worms are present. Diarrhea can also be caused by toxic insecticides, and the droppings can resemble those caused by salmonellosis.

Treatment: Serious cases must be injected by a veterinarian with 0.5 ml oxytetracycline-t, repeated after 24 and 48 hours. In addition oral administration of chlortetracycline-plus must be given via the drinking water twice daily for five days; after the first five days no medications for two days; or an individual treatment of one furazolidone-plus capsule per bird per day; or one to two capsules of chlortetracycline per bird per day. Naturally, the cote must be thoroughly cleaned and disinfected. The birds should receive no grit during the course of treatment. The veterinarian should advise appropriate post-treatment that should be followed conscientiously.

Ectoparasites

These are parasites that live on the outside of the host's body, in contrast to endoparasites, which live inside the body. There are only a few kinds of lice and mites that infest pigeons: The long louse (*Columbicola columbae*), the small louse (*Goniocotis compar* or *Coloceras damnicorne*), the quill or feather mite (*Falculifer rostratus*), the itch, body mange, or depluming mite (*Cnemidocoptes laevis, var. gallinae*), and the red mite (*Dermanyssus gallinae*).

Long Louse: Found on the flight feathers and guard feathers of the whole body, long lice do not cause many problems, since they feed on feather scurf and do not damage feathers as was previously thought. Sick birds that are not able to control the lice are susceptible to heavy infestations. Young birds may have particular problems with this louse. The lice can easily be seen by spreading the wings. In heavy infestations the lice may be seen on the neck, head, and back.

Small Louse is small and round. It also feeds on feather scurf but does more damage than the long louse, causing much irritation (prickling, burning). The small louse must be controlled. It is found on the underside of the guard feathers on the throat. Free flight helps to keep these lice under control, since they are light-shy.

Feather or Quill Mite is the most important of the mites. It sits on the feather shaft of the flight feathers, especially the wider ones. It does not destroy feathers but causes much irritation. Feather mites can be best seen if the wing is held up to the light; they appear as small black specks on the sides of the shafts.

Itch Mite is fortunately not as common as it once was. These mites cause feathers to fall out and are very dangerous. They burrow through the feather shaft into the follicle. If fallen feathers have a swollen root, probably itch mites are the cause. The feather shaft swells and the feather is shed. Small pale spots appear on the undersides of feathers on the breast, wings, back, and neck.

Red Mite will not be found by examining a pigeon. During the day the mites hide in nooks and crannies in the cote and come out at night to suck blood. The mite causes irritation and damage through bloodsucking (hence the red color). To find the mites, you must inspect the cote during the evening or night, especially on and under the perches, where they will be seen as tiny, fast-moving red vermin.

Other parasites such as fleas and ticks seldom infest pigeons.

A pigeon should not suffer from a single parasite and we must ensure that these are destroyed.

Control of Ectoparasites: Insecticides are used to control ectoparasites, as well as flies and mosquitoes. The insecticides we use should destroy the parasites, but should not be dangerous to the pigeons. If the wrong insecticide is used or if the insecticide is used improperly, there is danger of poisoning the pigeons. The instructions on the package must be carefully followed.

The use of insecticides should be kept to a minimum. They are poisonous, and can cause pigeons to suffer toxic symptoms. In small doses, you may not see these symptoms, but the bird will be unable to reach top condition. In severe cases of overexposure, the bird will die.

Insecticides in use at the present time include dietreen, pyrethrum, or carbaryl; read the package label carefully before you buy. Residual insecticides (which work over long periods)are not recommended; they are more likely to cause poisoning.

Endoparasites

These are parasites that live inside the body. The most important endoparasites in pigeons are the roundworm, the threadworm, and the fluke.

Roundworms: The fully grown roundworm lives in the small intestine and is approximately 2 inches (5 cm) in length. The female worm can lay hundreds of thousands of tiny eggs, which are visible only under a microscope.

The eggs are excreted in the pigeon's droppings. Outside, the eggs require 14 days to become infectious; they must first ripen. Any eggs taken up by another bird in this 14-day period will not develop.

However, if a pigeon takes up eggs that are ripe (that is, those that have lain on the ground for 14 days or more), larvae will hatch from the eggs in the intestines. The larvae burrow into the walls of the intestine, where they stay for some time. The exact length of time is unknown, but believed to be about 15 days until the worms develop into their adult form.

The amount of damage caused by these worms depends on the degree of infestation. A single worm will not do much damage, if any, but a large number of worms blocking the alimentary canal can prove fatal. Properly, a pigeon should not have a single parasite in its body. The worms take a large proportion of nutrients from the pigeon and produce toxins that prevent normal digestion. The food does not stay in the intestine long enough to be digested, and this results in diarrhea.

Pigeons suffering from worm infestations cannot come into top form; they molt badly and perform poorly. In slight infestation, little or nothing will be apparent to the observer, but in serious or protracted infestations, the pigeon will lose weight, have diarrhea, molt badly (failing to cast downfeathers), and quickly fatigue.

Should worms about 2 inches (5 cm) long be seen in the droppings, you can be sure that the bird has a roundworm infestation, but in most cases the worms are not seen. The droppings should be examined by a veterinarian, who will be able to find the eggs with the help of a microscope.

An infested bird is treated with a vermicide, and since not all larvae are affected by the various treatments, a further treatment is required about 21 days later.

To prevent worm and other infestations, strict hygiene in the pigeon cote is required. Floors, boxes, and perches should be kept very clean. The worm eggs are very resistant and difficult to eradicate. They require a damp medium at normal temperatures in which to ripen; in times of warm, damp weather, the worm eggs stand a much greater chance of ripening. They are less resistant to dryness. To destroy the eggs, the best method is to

How to Keep Pigeons Healthy

sanitize the floor with a blow torch. To prevent infestation in the cote the pigeons should have their food served in clean containers.

Confined birds are more susceptible to worm infestations than free-flying ones, and the chances of reinfestation are greater. It is advisable to place a mesh floor in aviaries, so that the droppings fall through. The floor must be cleaned well at least once a week. Strange pigeons can bring worm infestations into the cote, so these must be driven away immediately.

To protect your pigeons against worm eggs, a regular control and prophylactic treatment should be given, for example before the breeding season.

If you do the control through your club (during the show season), the chances of infestation will be greatly minimized. Your veterinarian or health laboratory will be able to carry out the examination for eggs.

Threadworms: As the name implies, threadworms are as thin as a thread and hardly visible to the naked eye. The threadworm lives in the walls of the intestines and, in spite of its much smaller size, can do more damage than the roundworms.

The worm eggs require similar conditions to those of roundworms to ripen—that is, a certain amount of time in a damp medium before they are taken up by a pigeon and can develop further.

The symptoms of threadworm infestation are similar to those of roundworms. The preventive measures, hygiene, and examinations are also similar. Some vermicides will work only against roundworms and not threadworms.

Intestinal Flukes: The intestinal fluke (named liver fluke in other animals), occurs only in grassy areas, especially on sloping banks of rivers, canals, or ditches. The pigeon can become infested only if it eats infested snails that live in such areas.

The parasite is flat and almost as wide as it is long. It lives on the walls of the intestines and holds on tightly by biting, causing much damage. Blood vessels are destroyed and hemorrhage occurs.

This can be so serious that a pigeon can die from blood loss in a few hours. A pigeon may be progressively infested by eating snails and die suddenly, giving the impression that it has been poisoned.

This endoparasite is the most dangerous of all the intestinal parasites. The eggs are also passed out in the droppings. An immediate treatment is absolutely essential.

To prevent further infestations, do what you can to keep the birds from areas where the infested snails are. This is a difficult task. Take care that the young birds do not fly out with the adults (and visit the same places). Let the older birds out late, so that they cannot fly too far away.

Control of Endoparasites: Control of endoparasites is not as simple as the control of ectoparasites. Roundworms are so large that they can be seen with the naked eye; if a worm about 2 inches (5 cm) long is seen in the droppings, it is not too difficult to diagnose. But pigeons can also suffer from a roundworm infestation without your knowledge. Threadworms, flukes, and coccidia are too small to see without a microscope. As these parasites live in the intestine and pass their reproductive products via the droppings (eggs from worms and oocysts from coccidia), the droppings can be microscopically examined for diagnosis.

To control, we must give the bird a medicine to destroy the parasites. There is a danger that the medicine itself will be absorbed by the bird, thus making it sick; there is also a risk that the normal intestinal flora will be harmed. Fortunately, there are medicines for worms and for coccidia that are quite safe. Before using any of these treatments, obtain advice from a veterinarian who is expert in this field.

Regular fecal examinations for the presence of parasites is very useful; usually you cannot see if a bird is infected or not, and when you can see it, it is often too late. As a good pigeon fancier you should always ensure that your birds are free from all parasites.

Understanding Your Pigeon

Pigeons in the Wild

With the exception of the polar regions, the order or group of pigeons and doves (*Columbiformes*) is to be found all over the world, and has its greatest development in the Oriental and Australasian regions. Pigeons and doves (the names are interchangeable and have no particular scientific meaning) vary in size; of the nearly 300 wild species there are those which are a little larger than a sparrow, and others which reach the size of a ptarmigan. Some are plump fruit-eaters; others, small and dainty seed-eaters. The birds also vary in their choice of habitat, which include humid, dense rain forest, dry desert and semi-desert areas, and the temperate regions of Europe and North America. They vary in their coloration, too, from blue-gray and white with a striking red patch on the breast (bleeding heart pigeon, *Gallicolumba luzonica*), to milky white with black flight feathers and a black-tipped tail (nutmeg pigeon, *Ducula bicolor*), and various species with plumage in soft, delicate shades of gray, pink, blue, and yellow.

But although there are contrasts, there are as many similarities among the various species of this family. Characteristic of all pigeons and doves is the whirring sound produced by their wings on take-off. Another unique characteristic of Columbiform birds is their ability to suck up water through their short beaks without raising their heads (they take water in a long draft, as horses do). Also, the bill has a swollen cere at the base which covers the nostrils.

Pigeons and doves feed mainly on seeds, berries and other fruits, and also insects. They may travel several miles from the nest in search of food for their young. They possess a fairly muscular body, thickly beset with feathers which are, however, loosely attached in the skin and are downy at the base. (This is why the feathers of a dead pigeon fall out easily.) When resting, the pigeon doesn't tuck the head under the wing but pulls it down between the shoulders.

All pigeons and doves are monogamous and proverbially "loving" to their mates. Their nests (see page 56) are flimsy affairs, consisting of not more than a few twigs laid loosely in the bough of a tree. The clutch is very small, usually just two eggs (see page 56). They are most often a silvery-white, but lightly colored or even brown. In the majority of the species, both cock and hen build the nest (see page 56) and share in the incubation of the eggs, the hen sitting during the day. The incubation period (see page 38) varies from 14 to 19 days, and the young are born with closed eyes. They stay another 12 to 20 days in the nest and are fed with a substance known as "pigeon-milk" — partially digested food from the parents' crops, as well as cheesy curd-like pieces of the crop's lining (during the incubation period the lining of the pigeon's crop thicken).

Breeding Behavior

Pairing

With the majority of pigeon breeds, it has been determined that it is the hen who decides whether a nodding, parading cock will make a suitable mate. At the beginning of the breeding season, the cock will start his nodding head movements, even if there are no hens in the vicinity. A sexually ripe hen will usually greet an approaching cock also with a nodding head. What takes place thereafter is fascinating to observe. As soon as the hen has acknowledged the head nodding cock (by head nodding herself), the cock will peck himself intensively behind the wings. If the female remains interested, she will reach her head forward, usually before the cock has withdrawn his beak from his wings. Then the female quickly moves closer to the male and he usually makes his mating call; the female fans her tail out. The cock then offers his open beak to the hen. Both birds rub their beaks together and the hen puts her beak inside that of her future mate, who feeds her with regurgitated food — or goes through the motions of doing so. "Billing and cooing" is a

Understanding Your Pigeon

Some enemies of the pigeon: Clockwise from bottom left: rat, hawk, owl, and raccoon.

very important part of the courtship ceremony, as well as head nodding (the beak may be held at an angle of 85–90° to nearly horizontal). Nodding also occurs when the birds meet each other in the nest, and during mating. As the head nodding often occurs near the nest site, it is thought that this behavior is a communication between the sexes about where the nest will be situated. The cock in particular likes to conduct his courtship near a pro- spective suitable nesting site; even more often he likes to fly directly to one of the chosen nesting sites. Studies of wild pigeons show that a hen will not readily mate with a cock unless he is in firm possession of a nesting site.

In the wild, as well as in captivity, it regularly happens that the two young nestlings (which are usually of both sexes) are attracted to each other and carry out pseudo-courtship rituals; after a few months they may even actually copulate. The mat- ing drive can be very strong. This can be seen if we separate the pair in two adjacent cages. At the high point of the breeding season, the two birds are introduced and copulation may take place without much "foreplay." Throughout this period it has been observed that even the usually important "bill- ing" takes second place.

Nest and Clutch

The hen lays two eggs in the nest. In the wild, pigeons may sometimes use the old nests of other birds. What the pigeons look for first is *safety*. A hen will not lay her white or cream-colored eggs in a nest that is not situated in a safe place. In the wild, pigeons choose holes, crevices, and ledges that are difficult for predators to reach. In order to increase the safety, many pigeons breed in colonies, so that they can warn each other if danger threatens and approaches.

The nest is built from small twigs, roots, grass, hay, and sometimes leaves that are collected by the male and put together by the female; she is the architect. When the nest is finished, the hen will lay her first egg during the evening. In the wild, the cock will stay some distance from the nest to avoid attracting predators to the "nursery." The female stays on the nest, but should she have to leave it, she will cover the eggs with twigs and moss to protect them from the eyes of unwelcome visitors.

In most cases, the cock will assist with the brooding, but the work is not equally shared. The cock will usually take over the brooding by midday, but the hen is usually back in the nest by mid- afternoon, and she continues the brooding through the night. It is clear that the hen does most of the brooding!

When the young have hatched they are fed within the first hour. The chick's beak is taken into that of the parent, who regurgitates the food. This "pigeon-milk" is given to the young for the first few days, but after the fourth or fifth day, they will begin to take more solid food. About half the time the young spend in the nest they must eat the same food that the parents have eaten. During the feeding of "pigeon milk" the parent ensures that nothing is lost; by each regurgitation of food it tries to make the nestling take as much as possible. This is not always possible, and some of the food remains in the parent's throat. This is reswallowed and will be regurgitated and offered the nestling again and, if necessary, again, so that there is no waste.

Understanding Your Pigeon

A pigeon feeding its young.

The Defense of the Nest and Young

The behavior of various pigeon species, although similar, varies somewhat. In general, depending from where the enemy approaches, the pigeon will stand perfectly still, with its plumage held flat against its body. If the enemy approaches from below, the pigeon will hold its body almost vertically; if the enemy approaches from above, the pigeon's body will be held almost horizontally. Pigeons are often warned by other pigeons when danger approaches; they fly with noisy clapping of wings to create an alarm. If danger occurs at night, a pigeon may panic and blindly fly off.

Usually the danger must be large and close before a pigeon will fly off the nest. It usually stays in its instinctively assumed position in the hope that the enemy will not notice it. Should the risk be too great, however, it will run or fly away. Pigeons avoid places where they have experienced danger.

Feeding Behavior

There are three groups of pigeons, depending on their methods of feeding; these are:
• Pigeons that obtain their food in trees and shrubs.
• Pigeons that obtain their food in trees and shrubs *and* on the ground.
• Pigeons that obtain practically all their food on the ground.

The pigeons from the first group live mainly in the tropics and subtropics and include all fruit-eating pigeons: many *Columba* species, the mountain dwellers of the genus *Gymnophaps* and the long-tailed pigeons of the genus *Reinwardtoena*. Their food consists of a rich assortment of fruit, flower petals, buds, young twigs, pods, etc. A few species will try slugs and snails (for example the white-crowned pigeon, *Columba leucocephala*, from the West Indian Islands, Florida, the Bahamas, the Antilles, Cuba, etc.) Most of these species will descend to the ground to obtain grit and other minerals. Only in times of adversity or during the breeding season will these species seek food on the ground.

The second group of pigeons (that feed both in the trees and on the ground) is very large. With the help of the long, pointed beak, they seek delicacies among the leaves. As far as I know, the Marquesas ground pigeon (*Gallicolomba rubescens*), from the Marquesas Islands of Fatuhuku and Hatutu, also uses its feet to search for food, as do all gallinaceous birds (poultry, grouse, pheasants, etc.); this fact, by the way, was discovered in an aviary. Most pigeons swallow food items whole, whether they be seeds, pieces of bread, cheese, snails, berries, or other kinds of fruit. Many African pigeons also take flying termites, as the extinct American passenger pigeon also did. In 1919, Whitman reported that an aviary-kept specimen of the American passenger pigeon pulled an earthworm from the ground and fed it to its squabs.

It is well known that during the breeding season many pigeons quickly adapt to available food and are then not at all particular; indeed, they may take food that is strange to them, especially if they see other birds eating it. The proverb, "What the peasant does not recognize, he will not eat" is often not appropriate to pigeons. Young pigeons will peck at practically anything that looks edible. If it is not edible the pigeon may hold the item in its beak until something edible is found.

Understanding Your Pigeon

Drinking, Bathing, Sunbathing, and Preening

Most pigeons drink freely several times a day. It has long been believed that fruit pigeons do not require water, but I have personally seen various wild species drinking in the evenings before they go to roost. It is often stated that the African Ringdove (*Streptopelia roseogrisea*) can go for months without a drink, but it is extremely doubtful if this is true. In 1982 I observed this species in the wild at various waterholes, and they gave me the impression that they are "heavy drinkers." Most captive pigeons will drink after a good feed and evidence suggests that wild pigeons behave similarly.

I know of only one species — the Australian crested pigeon *(Geophaps lophot*es) — that drinks heavily before "dining." Diamond Doves and many members of the genera *Columba* and *Streptopelia* drink before they feed their young. At this stage the youngsters take "normal" food *and* crop milk; in other words, the young are somewhat older. If a domestic pigeon goes without water for about a half hour after feeding, and needs to feed its youngsters, it will be restless and will not feed them. If water is then supplied, the parents will take a few long sips, then feed their offspring. It is probable that this also applies to wild pigeons.

Pigeons suck water and do not scoop it up like most birds (as we can see with chickens). The only exception is the tooth-billed pigeon (*Didunculus strigirostris*), which scoops up its water. The thirstier the bird, the deeper the beak is immersed in water! Pigeons usually drink from the bank. D. Goodwin encountered what he thought was the same Wood Pigeon four times in different places, landing on the water just like a duck; when the bird realized where it was, it took off quickly, without drinking. Perhaps a reflection on the water surface had induced the bird to make an unusual landing. There are, however, several kinds of pigeon that will actually stand in shallow water while drinking.

Many, though not all members of the genera *Columba, Streptopelia, Treron, Zenaida,* and others, like to shower in the rain. The bird lies partially on one side, supported by one wing while the other is held open, so that the rain falls on its flanks and under the wing. The rest of the plumage is also held in a position to catch the rain. Pigeons may also bathe in a pool or water puddle; the wings are then spread open over the water surface and the water is scooped over the plumage by movement of the head and wings. Afterwards the bird will retire to a sunny spot (often on a ledge) to dry its feathers. Here it will also spread its wings.

The Australian Diamond Dove does not bathe.

Sunbathing is also popular among pigeons and is done in the same way as a water bath — i.e., with outspread wings, and at an angle. The tail is also fanned out and is used as a weight to adjust the balance. I have seen pigeons that spread both wings as well as the tail during sunbathing, but only in the genus *Streptopelia.* After a time, the wings are pulled back into position and the whole plumage is puffed out. This is a favorite time for birds to engage in feather preening.

Some species enjoy an earth bath or sand bath (for example: the Spotted Ground Dove, *Metriopelia exciliae*). They do this frequently on hot days. Diamond Doves, however, just like to lie on the ground with spread wings; they are not taking an earth bath.

Feather preening is carried out similarly to that of other birds. The feathers are not cleaned with oil from glands like in some birds, but a big role is played by the feather powder, which is applied into the plumage to make it waterproof.

Pigeons remove dirt from their eyes by opening and closing the third eyelid, then rubbing the area against the shoulder. Head and beak are cleaned with the feet, which reach directly to the appropriate spot and not, as in most birds, over the wings.

Some movements made by pigeons arouse our curiosity. The *vertical stretch* often occurs. With wings held out, the head and tail are drawn down, and one of the feet is stretched backwards. Directly after this stretching of the foot, the wing on the same side is stretched. I believe the purpose of this stretching is to exercise the many muscles and to keep them in working order, just as we stretch ourselves for relaxation. Pigeons also stretch the body to flutter the wings, usually to dry out wet feathers; this, however, is unrelated to the vertical stretch.

Pigeons sitting in the sun or at roost do not tuck the head under the wing, but hold it tightly against the breast; frequently the plumage is fluffed out, especially in sick birds. A healthy bird at roost usually (with the exception of youngsters) stands on one foot, while the other is drawn up into the plumage. In sunny weather and after a water bath, pigeons like to lie down on their belly.

Social Behavior

Important aspects of social behavior of pigeons have already been revealed in discussions of feeding, nesting, and breeding.

Although the splendid song of birds has led to poets' writing about birds through the centuries, pigeons are rarely mentioned. Pigeons have a very limited "vocabulary." Most of them "coo" with the neck stretched. This cooing and other calls are used for many purposes, for example: contact, drawing of attention to certain things, attracting, or appeasing a partner, etc. There is little variety in the calling; for example, many nesting calls are similar to contact calls. Even the mating call is difficult to distinguish from the others; usually it is somewhat quieter, softer and "more loving." In birds of the *Columba oenas* variety, for example, the voice is barely audible.

If a bird is in pain or is fearful, the call can change to a "growling," gasping, or "yearning" tone that can be written as "oerh" or "ierh"; the strength of the tone depends on the size of the bird, but most pigeon breeds have similar tones. Really frightened pigeons will make this call frequently and end it with a sort of cry.

Defense Behavior

The bird spreads the feathers and the tail and raises one or both wings. This stance is usually taken if the bird is attacked while near or on the nest, or if special danger threatens and the bird wants to "shock" the intruder.

You can observe some pigeons, including the rock dove and its wild friends in town and village, suddenly thrusting their heads forward as if to stab at a rival. This gives the impression of an invitation to fight and is a good method of defense. In most cases, fighting does not occur and, after a couple of head stretches, the birds go peacefully about their business.

Head Nodding

This behavior is common among all the species I know, and is used as part of the courtship ceremony. It is extensively used by males to impress females to which they are sexually attracted. But some species also use this behavior to instill fear into a partner (or an enemy), or as a means of defense. During this nodding, the bird appears to be looking directly into the face of its partner. In most pigeon species, when the head is lowered, certain color patterns on the nape become clearly visible. At the same time, the pigeon lets out its characteristic cooing.

Depending on the species, the beak can nearly touch the ground or the breast as, for example, in the crowned pigeons; in this case, the crest appears as a large fan. In crowned pigeons there are no characteristic neck colors that are exposed during the head nodding. In case the crest is not impressive enough, the wings are lowered towards the ground and spread forward and the tail is fanned out. During the display an obvious contraction of the pupil occurs, which shows up the very colorful iris.

The spreading of the tail like a decorative fan is carried out by all pigeon species during the head nodding. The tail is usually raised upwards (as with most *Geopelia* species). The tail may be spread (as in the Rock Dove and the majority of fancy pigeons), even before the rest of the courtship is carried out. Possibly this short spreading of the tail originally arose as an impulse to escape; in many instances when the bird is in danger, it indeed will spread its tail before flying away.

In addition to the universally observed tail fanning and head nodding during courtship, some species of pigeons have also been known to also raise one foot.

Flying Behavior

There are various types of flight behavior that have not been studied for some species. Such flying, however, is obviously different from normal flight; the bird looks larger because of outspread wings; the movement of the bird is more stately, with more wing clapping. The up and down "clapping flight" is alternated with an up and down glide with outspread tail. Such a display is made above the mate, so that the markings on the underside of the tail are clearly visisble. Such flight in the courtship season is obviously correlated with the sexual drive of the pair. For example, it has been verified (Goodwin) that this flight behavior in domesticated pigeons occurs:

1. when the cock sees another pigeon flying;
2. when he sees his mate or another pigeon performing this flight behavior in the immediate area;
3. when he is at the point of flying away or returning to his cote after foraging for food, or after being transported away from his cote and he is forced to fly back to his cote "under his own steam";
4. when he flies in company with his mate;
5. immediately after copulation (in only 40% of the studied cases).

The Drooping of the Wings

Sexually excited pigeons frequently allow their wings to sag; that is, with the flight feathers somewhat separated and the whole wing partly opened. In this situation, many species clearly show the markings on their back.

The Feathers

The plumage of a pigeon is very efficient and wholly suited to its function. It is light and strong, protects the bird from inclement weather and skin injury, and helps in the regulation of its body temperature. Plumage insulates against heat in summer and against cold in winter.

We can classify the feathers into three types: flight feathers, contour feathers, and down feathers. The flight feathers consist of primary and secondary flight feathers and tail feathers. Flight feathers have a strong shaft that runs to the end of the feather. The feathers have a wide and a narrow side. Along the feathers run a series of barbs that interlock by tiny hooks; this gives the feather a solid appearance. The shaft originates from a follicle in the skin that can be compared with a human hair follicle. The feather develops in the feather follicle, which is surrounded with blood capillaries, so that the necessary nourishment for feather growth can be supplied. The base of the shaft is called the calamus, which has a round orifice through which the nutrients can be passed to the growing feather. When the feather is fully grown, this orifice closes up.

Contour feathers are very similar in construction to the flight feathers, but the shaft is not so strongly developed and is softer towards the tip. Contour feathers streamline the bird during flight and protect against wind and rain. They cover all parts of the wings and body that are in contact with the outside air.

Down feathers have a very short shaft that barely

projects from the body of the bird. The barbs are fully developed, but are not attached by hooks and are somewhat in disorder. These feathers insulate the bird's body.

The feathers are not distributed evenly over the body, but occur in so-called "feather fields." From the lower mandible a feather field runs into the breast, where it divides into two feather fields, one on either side of the breastbone. These join near the ears and then run down to the tail. There are no feathers at the jointed parts of the wings and the legs. A feather field runs over the head to the tail, stopping at the tail base; another pair of fields runs from the thighs into the tail feathers.

The Molt

Every year, pretty well all of a pigeon's feathers are renewed. This process usually runs from the summer (mid-July) to the beginning of the winter (mid-December).

The molt begins with the primary flight feathers. As soon as the new feather is three-quarters grown, its corresponding old feather will fall out. The feathers fall out from both wings at the same time. Not all feathers are dropped together, as this would render the bird unable to fly. After the ten primary flight feathers have been molted, the secondaries begin to molt. The number of secondaries that molt each year varies from pigeon to pigeon. Some may molt just two or three a year while others may molt all of them. At approximately the same time as the flight feathers are molted, the tail and contour feathers are molted also. The tail feathers are dropped in pairs, starting with the innermost ones. They are not dropped evenly, but so that as much flight surface as possible is available at all times. Of the large feathers, the outermost tail feathers are the last molted.

The feathers of head, neck, breast and belly are

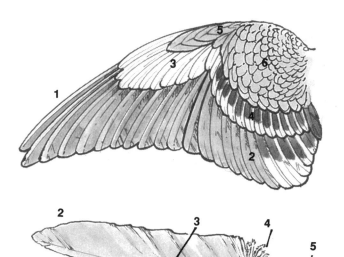

Top: Parts of the wing.
1. primaries
2. secondaries
3. primary coverts
4. secondary coverts
5. alula
6. lesser wing coverts

Bottom: Parts of the feather.
1. outer web of vane (vexillum)
2. inner web of vane
3. rachis or shaft
4. down feathers or fluff
5. quill or calamus

Understanding Your Pigeon

molted simultaneously with the feathers of the wings and the contour feathers, sometimes in whole groups together, so that a bird may occasionally have bald patches, even a bald head.

Down feathers are molted during most of the year. You can assess the condition of a bird by the quality of the down feathers. If the pigeon is not well, the down feathers, particularly those around the ears, are stiff and hard, and do not come easily from their follicles. This can be a result of disease, an inadequate diet, or an overextended breeding season that left the bird no time to prepare for the molt. It is therefore advisable to stop breeding birds after the end of June.

Molting is not a sickness, as some fanciers believe, but a natural process, that should run normally in healthy birds. Young pigeons replace their juvenile plumage in 30–35 days; under normal conditions this should pose no problems.

During the rearing of the young, usually about the 14th day, they sometimes receive inadequate food for a few days, because the cock is ready to start a new brood. This can later lead to so-called "growing stripes" in the plumage. One can then see, especially on the flight feathers, that a disturbance has occurred during feather growth. Should the cock neglect his duties because of a new nesting drive, both parents should be locked in with the young until the first egg of the next clutch is laid.

A pigeon in poor condition may have problems with new feather growth, manifesting itself in "blood feathers" and "tube feathers."

"Blood feathers" can occur when the blood vessel in the feather follicle is damaged and blood flows freely into the shaft. Sometimes this will right itself; never pull such a feather out, as it may not be replaced by a better feather and the bird is likely to lose a lot of blood.

"Tube feathers" occur when the membrane around the growing feather will not break. The barbs cannot then take their normal position and the feather remains "rolled up." "Tube feathers" are usually the result of chronic illness, inadequate diet, or generally poor condition of the pigeon.

Above left: The double-crested priest is originally from northwest and central Germany.
Above right: The monk pigeon, also originally from Germany, is a toy pigeon.
Center left: The ice pigeon, a toy pigeon from Germany.
Center right: The archangel. Its name is derived from the French "*Arc-en-ciel*", meaning "rainbow."
Below left: The Old German Moorhead.
Below right: The Lahore, from India.

Breeds of Pigeons

It is obviously impossible to describe in this book all the pigeon breeds (over 200), especially since each breed may have a number of colors and markings. A good example is the Modena, which has about 160 color and marking varieties!

In pigeons, there are four main colors: red, black, blue and brown. Lighter shades are also possible: yellow, liver color, blue-silver, and earth-colored (khaki).

Colors can be glossy or flat. Breeds such as color pigeons (Modenas, Florentines, archangels, etc.) and highfliers and tumblers are known for their deeply glossy colors.

Wattle Pigeons

The *carrier*, one of the best known members of this group, is a tall bird with a long, strong neck, broad breast, long tail (which must not touch the ground), and extensive beak and eye wattles. Birds three years old or more can have beak wattles as large as walnuts. The breed originated in the East and is one of the oldest known breeds in Europe. In English literature it was referred to as the Moor in 1735, while Charles Darwin referred to it as being "too valuable to fly around." Darwin was convinced that the carrier was developed directly from the Persian post pigeon, and this is still thought to be the case. However, in spite of their ancestry, carriers are not the most proficient fliers. In the course of time, the breed has become heavier and birds 20 to 23 ounces (560–650 gm) are regarded as the ideal size for showing.

Colors of this breed include black, liver-brown,

Above: Bokhara trumpeters.
Below left: The Altenburg trumpeter is one of the many varieties deveoped in Germany in the later part of the 19th century.
Below right: The German double crested trumpeter.

red, yellow, white, and blue, with black borders to the wings.

The *barb* is smaller in build than the carrier, but with broad head. The wattles on the beak are not nearly as well developed, but the wide, carmine-red eye borders (which are thick on the outer edge, thin on the inner edge) are immediately obvious. Over the years, attempts have been made to breed the beak shorter. In spite of the differences in body size, the carrier and the barb are closely related. The barb comes in the same color varieties; it originated in India but has been improved in England.

The *Baghdad* varieties are also closely related to the carriers and also originated in the East. There are several types; the robust and proud *Nuremberg Baghdad* (sometimes called *lark* or *scandaroon*), which has a short beak, and the *Steinheimer Baghdad* and the *French scandaroon* (or *Baghdad*), with a straight beak. This last breed was used in the creation of the well-known *English magpie* (see page 73).

The *dragon*, an English breed, has deep-blue eye borders as a distinguishing feature. The beak is blunt; although many pigeons have a thicker lower mandible, both mandibles of the dragon are of similar thickness, which is significant in the showing of these birds. The beak wattles lie close to each other. The short feet are unfeathered, set fairly well back, and relatively wide apart. The eyes are robin-red.

Structure Pigeons

A rich variety of breeds falls under this category, which includes *fantails*, *Jacobins*, *frillbacks*, and *silkhair fantails*. All of these breeds have one thing in common: they originated in India or China, and were in the 16th and beginning of the 17th centuries introduced to Europe, especially England, Germany, and the Netherlands. Especially the nimble and energetic fantails and Jacobins were bred in Europe to their present forms. The present fantails

Breeds of Pigeons

Indian tail-marked black fantail.

European fantail.

from Europe and America are now unlike their counterparts from the East; they have a character of their own.

The *European, Indian*, and *American fantails* are recognized by their strong neck, carried well back, and the robustly spread tail, carried almost vertically, with approximately 30–32 feathers (sometimes as many as 42). (The Indian breeds have, like most pigeons, 12–14 tail feathers.) Fan-

Red ribbontail Indian fantail (cock).

tails occur in a single color, single color with markings, colored but with a white tail, etc. It is interesting to note that the birds walk on their toes. Should something excite them, they will make unusual trembling movements. An old English breed notes this trait in its name: broad-tailed shaker.

The *Jacobins* — one of the oldest breeds of domesticated pigeon — have, in the last two centuries, developed enormous collars (hoods). In this connection, it is interesting to know that the original 17th-century type from India is now to be seen in all its glory as the Old Dutch capuchine, which has a splendid collar that leaves the head wholly free.

Jacobins are usually "monkish," that is, they have a colored body, but the head, tail, and flight feathers are white. There are many color variations, such as red, black, yellow, blue with black bands, etc., but the most important feature of this breed is the well-developed collar that almost overwhelms the head. In Germany these birds are called *Perückentaube*, or *wig pigeons*. The large collar makes it difficult for the bird to see. Many breeders clip the collar short during the breeding season so that the birds can easily see to feed their young.

The *frillbacks* are more delicately built; there are colored varieties with feathered feet. Colors include black, blue-shimmer, red-shimmer, and yellow-shimmer. The frillbacks owe their name to the curled feathers of the upper wings. In my opin-

Jacobin.

ion, the best frills are to be seen in the red-shimmer and yellow-shimmer varieties.

The little *silkhair fantails* have a silky plumage; that is to say, the feathers resemble fine hair because the feather barbules are without hooks. This characteristic — which occurs in only a few breeds — is quite rare, although often found in fantails. Most birds have the silken feathers in the tail, while the remainder of the plumage consists of "normal" feathers. It is not a breed in the true sense.

Giant Pigeons and Meat Pigeons

These two groups are closely related. The *runts* and the *Montaubans* are very well-known giant pigeons. The latter is the smaller of the two breeds. The enormous runts have a wingspan of 37 to 39 inches (90–100 cm), and according to literature, were bred and eaten by the Romans. At present, it is thought that the breed originated in southern France, where they were bred from stock originating in Cairo, Egypt. The long form, long wings and tail, and the long, broad head are the most important characteristics. The eyes are pearl-colored and surrounded by a red border, but in white individuals, dark eyes have gray-black borders. It is understandable that these heavy birds, weighing sometimes

more than 3½ pounds (1.5 kg), are not the best fliers. The nest boxes should therefore be placed quite low. The Montaubans also originated in southern France and they have a scalp-cap. Both breeds are best kept in a roomy loft, with four or five pairs kept and bred together.

The *Romagnolles* (with feathered feet) and the *Sottobancas* (with naked feet) are very broad in form and belong to the giant pigeons.

The *Mondains* are very popular in France and Italy (from whence they originated) and can also be shown as meat pigeons. They are very robust in build, usually white in color (although other colors occur, including pied) and may have feathered or naked feet. This variety is also found in Asia Minor, India, and China. In the United States some slightly different forms are known, including the popular *American duchess*, which is similar to the Romagnolle and the *giant American crest,* which has a skull cap and can weigh a little over 2 pounds (1 kg).

The *Cauchois* is a splendidly colored and marked breed. With a long tail and tricolored feathers on its long wings, it is one of France's oldest varieties.

The *king*, the American meat pigeon, originated from crossings of many heavy breeds (runt, Mondain, Maltese, and homing pigeon), but is now a

Cauchois.

somewhat compact type. In addition to white and brown-silver colors, there are yellow, black, and red varieties, but these are lighter in weight than the white and brown-silver kings. The eye border is beetroot red.

The *Carneau* originated in the border regions of southern Belgium and France. It is still very popular in France as well as in the United States, where it is heavier, weighing more than 2 pounds (1 kg). There is a splendid deep gloss on the neck. The forehead is very prominent. The eye border is red, except for the black variety, which has a black to coral-colored eye border.

The European red Carneau; this breed started as a "field pigeon" on farms.

The *Maltese pigeons* also originated from meat breeds and, since they were crossed with French Baghdads, are regarded as show pigeons. At present, the neck and the legs are long and the body is short and squat. This squatness is further enhanced by the short, upright tail. The flight feathers are also short, so the Maltese cannot fly more than a few inches from the ground. The fancier who keeps this breed must provide a loft close to the ground.

The *Hungarian* or *Huhnscheck* is similar in markings to the Modena: the main flight feathers are always white. The body, resembling a chicken, is robust and proudly carried. The breast is broad and full and the belly well filled out. The wide back should be as short as possible.

The *Modena* is a very popular breed, especially in France, Asia Minor, India, and China. It is an excellent meat breed with a massive, heavy, and deep body and a relatively small head. Birds less than 2 pounds (1 kg) in weight stand no chance in an exhibition! The breast is so wide and deep that you require two hands to cover it. The shortish back is somewhat concave and very wide, running into the short, horizontally carried tail. The short legs stand wide apart and the feet are unfeathered, although the thighs and legs are lightly feathered. The upper legs are covered by the breast feathers, but sometimes the toes are also covered. This is a plus point for the deep belly. The back must be white in the blue, gray, and red-silver varieties. Breeders must ensure that the head is not too narrow and that the forehead is prominent. The eyes are dark in the white variety and orange-red in the other colors. The medium-length beak is rose-colored in the white variety; in the other color varieties the beak ranges from light to dark horn-colored. Self (single) colors include white, black, red, yellow, blue with black bands, gray and red-silver.

The *Polish lynx* (in my opinion, more handsome than the Hungarian and the Modena) originated in

Fairy swallow or blue, white-barred spot swallow.

Breeds of Pigeons

Poland and is a meat breed that has become the victim of its own beauty. Because of selective breeding for its handsome markings, the bird's size has suffered. Efforts are now being made to increase the size of the breed but to retain its beautiful markings. This breed has a broad and full breast, but the deep belly is absent. The short, wide back is somewhat convex and slopes slightly. The short, wide wings lie tightly and must cover the back well. The tail is wide and short; the legs are also short and unfeathered. The large head has a fairly broad and high forehead; the beak is long and dark-colored, except in the reds and the yellows, when it must be flesh colored. Other colors are black and blue.

Red, white-barred fairy swallow.

The various *fancy swallows* are originally from Germany but well known in this country. In 1873, Griffith and Hofheins exhibited the first fancy swallows at Buffalo.

The *Strasser* comes from Czechoslovakia, a country that does not have a great record in producing breeds of pigeons. But here we have a breed that is well known and loved worldwide and is frequently bred. This massive bird is short and naturally broad. What a pity that in some countries the size has been somewhat diminished. The broad, deep, and round breast is carried well forward. The broad back is usually short and somewhat inclined. The rather broad tail slopes away from the back and offers plenty of room for the folded wings. The legs

are short, strong, and unfeathered. The medium-long neck is robust, wide at the shoulders, and has a well-profiled throat. The head is large and rounded, the forehead prominent. The eyes are red to orange-red. The colors include black, red, yellow, and blue, with a deep-black band. There are also Strassers in these colors with white bands, as well as blue-silver, dark red, or yellow bands. There are other fascinating colors that we, alas, cannot cover in this short text.

Croppers

Whether the *croppers* originally came from Arabia to Europe is not definite, but it is a fact that Holland played a very significant role in the development of the different varieties, and already in the 17th century, near perfect specimens were known.

Croppers are known to fanciers as being especially lively; they quickly become tame and attached to their owner.

The *English pouter* is a splendid example of a cropper. It is bred as large as possible and must stand nearly vertically on its feet. The outstanding features of this breed are the enormously long legs and the total slenderness. The legs are the most demanding point in the standard for this breed and many faults can occur. The legs are situated so closely together that you can hardly look between them and they must be almost perfectly straight; only at the knees are they allowed to be a little bent.

The *French cropper* is a large, naked-legged cropper with a tall, elegant bearing. The body is very long and narrow. The carriage is as follows: ⅔ of the body in front of the legs and ⅓ behind. The outstanding features of this breed are the large, round balloon that sticks out bowlike from the breast bone and the bowlike thigh bones that extend out from the rump. Characteristically, if you look at the bird from above, you get the impression of three broken circles.

The *Dutch cropper* is probably the best known

Breeds of Pigeons

Dutch cropper. The distinguishing feature of all croppers is their ability to inflate their crops.

of the cropper varieties and a bird that has played a major part in the development of the other croppers. The heavily built cropper is rightly Holland's proudest and at the same time, oldest known breed. It is always peaceful, trusting, and nondemanding. The very thick feathering on legs and feet makes the bird appear as if it could never lose its balance. The straight neck, back, and tail line gives the bird a bearing that commands respect. The breed should not be too large. The long neck is decorated with a large balloon, which may not be spherical but may be low. Viewed from the side, the balloon runs into the breast and shoulders. The long, robust legs look short, because of the low bearing and the hidden knee joints. Because of the full feathering on legs and feet it is not possible to see between the legs. The eyes are mainly orange-colored.

The *Ghent cropper* comes from Belgium: it is a vigorous cropper with a short, compact body and thick feathering on the feet. The straight neck, the somewhat sloping back, and the horizontally carried tail give the impression of a concave line when seen from the side. These characteristics are very important standards of the breed. The neck is long but may also show no backward bow when the crop is inflated. The balloon is large and round and may not blow into the neck but must gradually run into

the body. Note well: through the near horizontal bearing and the upright neck, the balloon is inflated in a near vertical position. This gives the bird a unique appearance. The shoulders and the breast are very wide; the concave, wide, and short back makes for a very compact bird. The legs are medium-long and strong; the thick feathering on legs and feet must give an impression of unity and completeness. The eyes are dark in the white Ghent croppers and the *Dominicans*. In the other colors the eyes are yellow to orange-red. The Dominican has a white head and throat with a large, crescent-shaped white spot on the crop; the wing coverts with the exception of the shoulders, are white, as are the flight feathers, the lower part of the breast, the belly, the feathers on the legs and feet, and the underside of the tail; the rest is colored. The white underside of the tail is a characteristic of the Ghent cropper.

The *Voorburg shield cropper* is a breed for which we have to thank my friend, the late G. S. Th. van Gink, from Voorburg in the Netherlands. He developed a breed of white croppers with white wing markings — precisely the opposite of the markings seen on usual croppers. This fairly long, slender cropper is medium-sized, with an upright bearing. It is agile and lively. The breast is long and narrow, with a scarcely visible breastbone. The back is fairly hollow between the shoulders. The well-feathered tail may not touch the ground. The medium-length legs are placed centrally under the body and bent at the knees. The throat is long and bent backwards when the balloon is inflated. The balloon is more than medium-sized, nearly round, and sharply set off from the breast, so that the waist is emphasized.

The beak is fairly long, robust, and flesh-colored. The eyes are dark, with a small, flesh-colored border. The bird has wholly white markings, except for the upper wings on the outer 7–10 flight feathers. The colors must be as even and deep as possible; there is a splendid sheen, particularly in darker-colored birds. The breed is available in all regular pigeon colors.

The *Norwich cropper* originated in the Netherlands but has been maintained and bred to its present quality in England. The birds were introduced to England by Protestant Flemish refugees in 1550; until the 18th century the birds resembled the Holle cropper. At present, this breed is an upright, smooth-headed and smooth-footed pigeon with red to orange-colored eyes. There are 7–12 white feathers on the bend of the wing. An important caution: *never* allow croppers to take too much food and water at a time, as the possibility of "hanging crop" may arise, coupled with digestive problems.

The *Thuringian cropper* is a well-built breed with a pear-shaped crop, a light constriction at the breast, and a pointed cap. The *Silesian cropper* is also a robust bird with a pearlike crop that should overlap well into the breast, particularly on the upper side. All cropper varieties fly eagerly and frequently, and are best kept as free fliers. Both of these breeds originated in Germany.

The *Valencia cropper* originated in Spain. The crop of this temperamental breed does not inflate on the upper side. A good breed example is triangular in form.

Dwarf Croppers

Although the *English pygmy pouter* is one of the most popular, elegant, and friendly of the pigeon breeds, it is not known how its present body form was developed. When Sir John Sebright, the well-known pigeon fancier, died in the middle of the last century, several very small examples of the English pouter were found in his lofts — to the astonishment of many. It is no longer possible to say if these were the ancestors of the pygmy breed. The breed is identical to the English pouter, except smaller in form and thus possibly more elegant. The bird weighs about 3 ounces (86 gm) — about half that of its bigger relative.

The *Bruenner cropper* is of Czech origin, but developed to the present form in Germany. Unfortunately, it is not as small as it was 75 years ago; the white form was especially small. The present form, however, with its longer neck and slender waist, is much more elegant!

The *Holle cropper* (formerly also called the *Amsterdam pouter*) is a broad and short, but perfectly proportioned dwarf cropper. Everything is so round in this bird that it can be described as circular. The stance is fully horizontal. The neck is long and supple and bends over the back so far, that if we were able to lower a plumb line from the eye, it would touch the ground behind the bird's legs! But the head does look as though it is situated over the back. As the bird walks the head is gracefully moved forward and back. The eyes are dark in the white varieties, yellow to orange-red in the other colors (black, blue, pied, gray, red, yellow, blue-silver, red-silver). The bird is very lively and happily parades around. Low-quality specimens with a small breast, an overlong back, or a too slender rear end find difficulty in strutting around and try to maintain balance with the neck, often falling on the tail. This breed usually rears its own young successfully. Since 1924 there have been many enthusiastic breeders of this variety in England. Through imports of birds from the Netherlands after World War II the quality of the breed has improved immensely. Good stock also exists in the United States, and in recent years numerous birds of Dutch origin have been transported great distances to triumph in shows. Because of its amusing character and charming gait in the aviary and at the shows, the Holle cropper, which originated in northern Holland, has become one of the most loved pigeon breed all over the world; and rightly so!

Tumblers, Rollers, and Highfliers

Tumblers are so named because in flight they frequently and regularly tumble. Although it was supposed for a long time that this phenomenon was due to some form of epilepsy, it is now thought that it has something to do with a genetic defect in the birds' inner system of balance. At the present time, *good* tumblers have become quite scarce. This large group is split into those with long beaks and those with short beaks.

The rollers are closely related to the tumblers; through their exuberant tumbling and rolling in the air, they can be described as the artists of the tumbler family. Good rollers can perform backward somersaults over a distance of more than 33 feet (10 m) in full flight, seldom falling more than 13 feet (4 m). This rolling originates from the bird's attempts to touch its tail with the back of its head, which results in a whole rotation of the body. The revolutions of rollers should be concentric and evenly balanced. In addition, rollers can tumble in forward somersaults. Fanciers of these birds often work with 20 or more individuals, with the knowledge that, in flight, one bird will encourage the next. Once one bird begins to roll, the others will almost always immediately follow the leader — a breathtaking exhibition!

One of the many tumbler breeds is the yellow Hollander tumbler.

The highfliers owe their name to the fact that they are able to fly at high altitudes — so high, that they can be seen only as tiny specks in the sky. Tumblers and rollers can also fly very high.

The nun, which was known in Holland in early 1600, is also a well-known tumbler.

The *English long-faced tumbler* is bred with both feathered and unfeathered feet, is not sturdily built; the body is short, broad, and compact, but nevertheless gives an impression of strength, due probably to the soft, smart plumage. The breast is also broad and round in this breed, and carried forward. The head is bullet-shaped, with a very broad and high sloping forehead, and the skull gives the impression of being semicircular in shape. The large eyes which are set in the middle of the head, are silver-white. This breed is available in most colors and markings, so there is something for everyone's taste. In the 19th century the *English short-faced tumblers* were produced, but they never became as popular as the long-faced breed.

The *Danish tumbler* is an extremely elegant bird with a long neck, long wings and tail, a long cone-shaped beak, and long feet. The beak is a most important feature of the bird: an imaginary line drawn through the line of the two mandibles must run through the center of the pupil. The Danish tumbler is available in many colors and markings.

The *German long-faced tumbler* is a slender, elegant, medium-sized pigeon. A good specimen has a long, narrow head and a long beak. An imaginary line drawn between the tip of the beak and the highest point of the skull (which is behind the eyes) should be straight, and should not pass through the pink wattles at the base of the beak. The eyes have a sparkling white iris and a small pupil. In some color varieties, the eye borders should be fiery-red.

The *Komorner tumbler* or *Hungarian whitehead* is a small, compact pigeon with an elegant crest and short legs.

The *English short-faced tumbler* is a small pigeon with a wide breast that is carried proudly high. The standard requires that the breast be rounded on all sides. The short wings are tightly folded to the body and carried *under* the tail; the opposite is true in the English long-faced tumbler. American fanciers do not care for this characteristic and prefer birds with the wings carried above the tail. A notable feature is the shiny white iris; the eye is surrounded with a smooth border.

The *magpie* is a picture of elegance, with a slender body and upright bearing. The narrow breast is carried high and the back slopes sharply downwards, forming a straight line with the tail. The high-set wings lie loosely and rest on the tail. The pearl-colored eyes are decorated with a red border.

The *Birmingham roller* is a small, slim pigeon

Komorner.

English long-faced tumbler.

with a domed head and fiery eyes. This hardy breed, which comes in all of the tumbler colors, is excellent for beginners.

The *Belgian highflier* is a fairly long pigeon, with a long neck, a long breast (which should not stick out too much), a long sloping back and pearl-colored eyes. The beak is long, thin, and white. The *Dutch highflier* is somewhat more elegant in build.

The *Danzig highflier* is recognized by its skull cap and its owllike tail. This strange tail, which does not hinder its flight, is made up of 14 to 18 wide feathers, with so-called double feathers in the center (two feathers that emerge from the same quill).

Owls

Many popular varieties are contained in this large group of pigeons. Having a happy and affectionate personality, these pigeons are well suited to the novice.

The *Old Dutch owl* is an ancient, medium-sized breed from the Netherlands, with an elongated, not too narrow head. The greatest breadth is just in front of the eyes, which is also the highest part of the skull. The full breast is well-domed, has a well-

Breeds of Pigeons

The rare Berlin short-faced tumbler is an owllike pigeon, similar to the English short-faced tumbler.

developed jabot (a cascade of plumage down the front of the breast), is long-feathered and strong in build. The dark eyes are large and round, and give a lively impression. The legs are medium length. The whole body is white except for the shield, which must be intensely marked.

The *Oriental frill* (*satinette, blondinette, brunette, turbitein,* and *vizor*) is a breed which was originally bred by the Greeks and the Turks, but the Dutch and the English perfected it. The Oriental frill is a small, charming pigeon with a friendly manner. The bird stands low on its feet, has a somewhat squat body shape and has feathered feet. Specimens with light-colored head feathers have orange eyes, while those with darker feathers have white eyes. The jabot consists of a row of well developed feathers. Because of feeding difficulties resulting from the short beak, the young are usually transferred to foster care; personally, I find the Franciscan velvet shields most suitable for this task. To prevent confusion, it is worth noting that satinettes, blondinettes, brunettes, turbiteins, and vizors are all the same breed — in other words, Oriental frills each in a special color variety.

The *African owl* is the smallest member of the owl group. It was introduced to Europe from Tunisia in 1850. It is a very affectionate bird with an an outstanding appearance — a proud bearing, a spherical head, broad breast, well-developed jabot, broad shoulders, and short back. The beak is very short. An imaginary line drawn along the join of the two mandibles must go through the center of the eyes at a 45-degree angle. The eyes are large, placed in the middle of the head, and dark-colored in the white pigeons, orange in the light-colored varieties. For a long time breeders have tried to produce the *English owl* in as small a form as its African relative, but so far have been unsuccessful. This breed, with its longer head, has therefore retained a character of its own.

The *Italian owl,* whose name indicates its origin, is the owl with the longest unfeathered legs. The bird is far from sturdy, gives a chickenlike impression, and walks on its toes as though it were ready for action. The medium-length neck is bent very

Oriental frill satinette.

decoratively back, and the jabot should be soundly developed.

The *Chinese owl* has the most outstanding jabot of all the owls. The breed is especially popular in Germany, where it is bred to near perfection. Originally the breed came from Africa. This medium-sized owl, with a strong leaning toward the smaller

Breeds of Pigeons

types, is notable for its rich feathering. Its broad, wedge-shaped body (a typical feature of all the owls) stands on short, wide-apart legs. The bird viewed from the front gives the impression of a living ball of down.

The *Antwerp smerle*, from Belgium, is the largest of the owl breeds. The robust body is held horizontally. The legs are unfeathered; the jabot is large. The forehead is broad; the eyes are dark brown, the beak strong and wide.

The *German shield owl* is a short, broad, round, white owl with a proud bearing. The breed originated in Asia, but was perfected in Germany. This bird is very similar to the African owl, but has shield markings and a short, stumpy, flesh-colored beak. There are smooth-headed, point-headed and scallop-headed varieties.

The blue African owl; this breed is presently the smallest domestic pigeon.

Trumpeters

The trumpeter originated in Asia, but was already bred in Europe 200 years ago. The typical trumpeter has feathers on the feet and is capped. It is very popular in Germany.

The *Altenburg trumpeter* was already mentioned by John Moore in 1735, in his book *Columbarium,* and he noted especially the strong "wack-wack" throat call. The domed head is broad and the forehead is high. The eyes are light, pearl-colored; the white variety may have pearl-colored or dark eyes.

The *Bokhara trumpeter* probably originated in Persia, but was perfected in the town of Bokhara in the Soviet Union. This breed has a compact, broad, and robust build. The flat and broad head has a wide skull cap, which runs back into manelike feathering. On the forehead is a many-feathered rosette that is so large that the whole forehead, the crown, the eyes and the beak are concealed. This trumpeter's feet are heavily feathered. It is a shame that the "trumpeting" has been almost completely bred out of the foot-feathered breeds.

The *German double-crested trumpeter* is also noted for its heavy feathering on the feet. It is a robust breed with a somewhat upright bearing and a thick vertical crest that is well supported by the throat feathering. The rosette is oval. The eyes are orange, but darker in the white and silver varieties.

Color Pigeons

Nearly all breeds of *color pigeons* originated in Germany, usually with the help of crossings with other fancy pigeons; due to the unreliable communications between Thuringen, Saxony, and Silesia, countless local breeds were produced, not only for their handsome colors, but also for their tasty meat. All color pigeons are simple to keep and house, are prolific and can rear their own young.

The *priest* is noted for its totally white head and its flat-lying crest, which ends in a rosette at the sides and should not come above the cap. The priest carries a single beak rosette at the front and a little semicircle of feathers at the base of the bill that grows out over the beak. The feet are strongly feathered. There is also a clean-legged priest that is very popular in some parts of the world, but is seldom seen in the United States.

The *monk pigeon* is very similar to the priest,

and is a very good breed for beginners, provided the floor of the cote is kept dry and the interior is well protected from rain and wind. This breed should have regular free flight, which is good for its health and fertility.

The *Francanian velvet shield* has an elongated body. It is very suitable for free flying. It will live peacefully with other breeds. The beginner can find much pleasure with this breed, as its care poses no particular problems and it breeds readily, producing fast and good results. The breed is noted for the elongated, somewhat domed head, the flesh-colored, medium-sized, straight tail. The eyes are dark and the feet are red.

The *Swiss* or *crescent* pigeon was taken to Germany from Holland between 1655 and 1656 by the Frankfurt doctor, Georg Horst. The breed was brought to Holland from India by Dutch seamen.

Crescents are fascinating birds, not only because of their remarkable, beautiful breast pattern, but also because of their typical colors and the difficulty of breeding them, which has led to the bird's losing some of its popularity. The breed has a robust manner with strong breast and shoulders. The fairly long head must be rounded, with a domed forehead. The eyes are dark or orange. The long beak is light in the yellow crescent, horn-colored in the brown varieties. The bird has long and full foot feathering. The crescent (half moon) marking starts on the lowest part of the throat, and is 1¼ inches (3 cm) at its broadest.

The *ice pigeon* is available with or without foot feathering. Ice pigeons were developed from blue pigeons and the plumage was gradually lightened to give the present splendid ice blue color. The bird has a smooth head and short legs. There are several varieties. They have a dark beak and dark eyes, but there are varieties with orange eyes. Ice pigeons should not be washed for at least two weeks before showing, as the plumage powder will be removed, having an adverse effect on the color. This fatty powder is emitted from an oil gland situated above the rump. Just like water birds, the pigeons spreads the fatty substance over its plumage with its beak.

Archangels occur in two basic color groups — red and yellow. The wings are differently colored — for example, black-winged red; blue-winged yellow. The origin of the breed poses a puzzle; we think the black-winged red originated in Dalmatia/Illyria (Yugoslavia), and the other colors in southern Germany/Austria. There are about 24 varieties. Since the various color forms are difficult to achieve, they are probably better suited for experienced breeders. With their glossy plumage they are perhaps the best known fancy pigeons in the world.

Moorheads are among the oldest of fancy pigeon breeds; they were probably brought into Germany and Holland around 1660. In the first bird show in Dresden in 1869, the word *"Mohrenköpfe"* (Moorhead) was used to describe the breed, since at that time the varieties were mainly black. Later, the colors blue, red, and yellow were bred, so that the name "Moorhead" is no longer really appropriate. Moorheads have an individual, fairly surly manner, but are easy to handle when young. However, older specimens are more difficult to introduce to new accommodation. They fly particularly well, have an excellent sense of orientation, and forage well during free flight.

The *swift* came originally from the Middle East. The main feature of the breed is the long tail and long wings (sometimes with a span as much as 31 inches (80 cm). There are two varieties: one with a short beak and a small, round head, the other with a noticeably slighter build. The first variety is fairly popular in the United States but, in spite if its name and its large wings, it is not a very good flier, as the feathers are too long and loose.

The *Lahore* is a large, strong, but docile bird that originated in India. The Lahore is one of the most colorful of pigeons, with a wide breast and a somewhat domed, wide back. The tail is long and wide, the round head is short and wide, with a high domed forehead. The beak is medium length and should be white. The large, dark eyes are rimmed with a narrow red border.

Useful Addresses and Literature

American Bird Clubs

American Pigeon Fanciers' Council
  2617 S.E. 138th Loop
  Vancouver, WA 98684
  c/o Mr. Steve Holden, Audio-Librarian
American Dove Association
  P.O. Box 21
  Milton, KY 40045
American Federation of Aviculture
  P.O. Box 1568
  Redondo Beach, CA 90278
International Dove Society
  2507 3rd Avenue North
  Texas City, TX 77590

Veterinarian Assocation

Association of Avian Veterinarians
  P.O. Box 299
  East Northport, New York 11731

Magazines

American Pigeon Journal (Monthly)
  (covering: Fancy, Utility, Homing Pigeons, and
  Doves)
  P.O. Box 278-BT
  Warrenton, MO 63383
American Federation of Aviculture
  P.O. Box 1568
  Redondo Beach, CA 90278

Books

Goodwin, D.: *Pigeons and Doves of the World,
  Bulletin British Museum of Natural History*,
  London, and Ithaca, NY, 1970.
Levi, W.M.: *The Pigeon*, Levi Publishing Co., Inc.
  Sumter, SC, 1941, 1963.

Index

Numbers in *italics* indicate color plates.

Index

Perfect for Pet Owners!

PET OWNER'S MANUALS

Over 50 illustrations per book
(20 or more color photos),
72-80 pp., paperback.

AFRICAN GRAY PARROTS (3773-1)
AMAZON PARROTS (4035-X)
BANTAMS (3687-5)
BEAGLES (3829-0)
BEEKEEPING (4089-9)
BOXERS (4036-8)
CANARIES (2614-4)
CATS (2421-4)
CHINCHILLAS (4037-6)
CHOW-CHOWS (3952-1)
COCKATIELS (2889-9)
COCKATOOS (4159-3)
DACHSHUNDS (2888-0)
DOBERMAN PINSCHERS (2999-2)
DWARF RABBITS (3669-7)
FANCY PIGEONS (4044-9)
FEEDING AND SHELTERING
  EUROPEAN BIRDS (2858-9)
FERRETS (2976-3)
GERBILS (3725-1)
GERMAN SHEPHERDS (2982-8)
GOLDEN RETRIEVERS (3793-6)
GOLDFISH (2975-5)
GUINEA PIGS (2629-2)
HAMSTERS (2422-2)
LABRADOR RETRIEVERS (3792-8)
LIZARDS IN THE TERRARIUM
  (3925-4)
LONG-HAIRED CATS (2803-1)
LOVEBIRDS (3726-X)
MICE (2921-6)
MUTTS (4126-7)
MYNAS (3688-3)
NONVENOMOUS SNAKES (5632-9)
PARAKEETS (2423-0)
PARROTS (2630-6)
PONIES (2856-2)
POODLES (2812-0)

RABBITS (2615-2)
SCHNAUZERS (3949-1)
SHEEP (4091-0)
SNAKES (2813-9)
SPANIELS (2424-9)
TROPICAL FISH (2686-1)
TURTLES (2631-4)
WATER PLANTS IN THE
  AQUARIUM (3926-2)
ZEBRA FINCHES (3497-X)

NEW PET HANDBOOKS

Detailed, illustrated profiles (40-60
color photos), 144 pp., paperback.

NEW AQUARIUM HANDBOOK
  (3682-4)
NEW BIRD HANDBOOK (4157-7)
NEW CAT HANDBOOK (2922-4)
NEW COCKATIEL HANDBOOK
  (4201-8)
NEW DOG HANDBOOK (2857-0)
NEW DUCK HANDBOOK (4088-0)
NEW FINCH HANDBOOK (2859-7)
NEW GOAT HANDBOOK (4090-2)
NEW PARAKEET HANDBOOK
  (2985-2)
NEW PARROT HANDBOOK (3729-4)
NEW RABBIT HANDBOOK (4202-6)
NEW SOFTBILL HANDBOOK (4075-9)
NEW TERRIER HANDBOOK (3951-3)

CAT FANCIER'S SERIES

Authoritative, colorful guides (over
35 color photos), 72 pp., paperback.

BURMESE CATS (2925-9)
LONGHAIR CATS (2923-3)
SIAMESE CATS (2924-0)

PREMIUM SERIES

Comprehensive, lavishly illustrated
references (60-300 color photos),
136-176 pp., hardcover.

AQUARIUM FISH SURVIVAL
  MANUAL (5686-8)
CAT CARE MANUAL (5765-1)
COMPLETE BOOK OF
  BUDGERIGARS (6059-8)
COMPLETE BOOK OF PARROTS
  (5971-9)
DOG CARE MANUAL (5764-3)
GOLDFISH AND ORNAMENTAL
  CARP (5634-5)
HORSE CARE MANUAL (5795-3)
LABYRINTH FISH (5635-3)

GENERAL GUIDE BOOKS

Heavily illustrated with color photos,
144 pp. paperback.

COMMUNICATING WITH YOUR DOG
  (4203-4)
DOGS (4158-5)

FIRST AID FOR PETS

Fully illustrated, colorful guide, 20 pp.
Hardboard with hanging chain and
index tabs.

FIRST AID FOR YOUR CAT (5827-5)
FIRST AID FOR YOUR DOG (5828-3)

ISBN prefix: 0-8120

Order from
your favorite
book or pet store

BARRON'S